edexcel

advancing learning, changing lives

STUDENT GUID

Level 3

Coordinating editors: Elizabeth Swinbank and John Taylor

A PEARSON COMPANY

Introduction

About extended projects

If you are using this book, you will almost certainly be working for an Extended Project (EP) qualification, either as part of a Level 3 Diploma or as a stand-alone qualification equivalent to half a GCE A-level.

An EP is a major piece of individual project work, in which you have the opportunity to explore a topic or a question that is of particular interest to you. You will make an artefact, write a dissertation, put on a performance or carry out a laboratory or fieldwork investigation.

But what is meant by an *extended* project? An EP is not simply yet another piece of coursework. Rather, it should extend your knowledge and skills in ways that are challenging and new to you. The examiners responsible for the qualification have defined 'extension' in three ways.

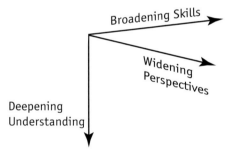

Deepening understanding

In your EP you should be exploring a topic or question in some depth, and you are likely to become a bit of an expert in that area. This is not just a matter of finding out some facts, but of thinking deeply about key ideas that relate to your Project.

Broadening skills

Your EP should give you an opportunity to learn how to do new things and to practise these, so that you develop some real expertise. These might be practical skills, thinking skills or research skills – or, most likely, a combination of all of these.

Widening perspectives

In doing your EP, you should aim to look beyond conventional subject boundaries and bring together ideas and skills from a range of areas. For example, try looking at a scientific topic from a historical perspective, or consider how political ideas might be explored through making art.

About this book

Before starting the main work for your Project, you will need to develop some general skills that you will use and demonstrate during your EP work. Chapters 1 and 2 of this Guide are about developing these skills of research and thinking. However, the book itself provides only the bare bones and it is likely that you will also engage in a wide range of activities relating to your particular line of learning, or subjects of study, and to the eventual topic of your Project. The CD-Rom that accompanies this Guide supports many such activities.

Chapter 3 of this Guide is where attention turns to your topic. Having developed a range of skills, and having explored some fruitful areas of interest, you should be in a position to decide what you are going to do for your EP and complete your Project Proposal Form. At this point, you will need to plan your Project in outline and begin to build up a record of your work (guidelines are provided in Section 3).

Chapter 4 takes you through the execution, or 'doing', of your Project, and shows how you can build up a written report one section at a time. As well as the general material in this Guide, you will probably also use other more specialised materials (e.g. from the CD-Rom) that relate to your own Project.

Finally, Chapter 5 takes you through the last stage of your EP, where you need to communicate your work using both a written report and a presentation, and respond to questions.

• Focused objectives

You need to have a clear idea of what your EP is setting out to do. Simply deciding to 'find out about *x*' or 'make *y*' will not lead to a high-quality EP. Developing a focused project proposal and a well-organised plan is addressed in Chapter 3 of this Guide.

• Independent learning

Under the supervision of your teacher/tutor, you will have a major responsibility for organising your time and making best use of the resources available. The guidance on planning in Chapter 3 of this Guide will help you here.

• Research based

Research is a key element of an EP. As well as developing your own ideas and skills, you should be finding out about the background to your Project, and learning how other people have addressed similar topics and questions. Chapter 1 of this Guide is about developing relevant research skills. For an investigation, you will also develop skills relating to laboratory or fieldwork and to data handling (the CD-Rom provides materials for this).

• **S**tructured outcomes

Just as your objectives need to be focused, the eventual output from your Project needs to be structured. A rambling report, in which you simply 'write about *z*', or a disorganised presentation, will not do justice to your work. CHapters 4 and 5 guide you through this aspect of your EP.

• **T**hinking skills

Not least, your EP is about thinking – that is, thinking critically about your own ideas and those of other people, analysing arguments for and against a particular point of view, and developing your own reasons and arguments in order to persuade others. These skills are the subject of Chapter 2 of this Guide.

Each section of this Guide includes the following features.

Key terms

Within the main text, some words are printed in **bold**. These are key terms relating to EP work, and are defined in the *Glossary* printed at the back of this book. You will probably need to use several of these terms in your Project.

Activities

The text includes many *Activities*. Some of these are intended for individual work, while others are designed for groups. It is likely that you will be asked to carry out some, though by no means all, of these activities in class or in private study time.

ACTIVITY 4: STRENGTHS AND WEAKNESSES OF WEB RESOURCES

List the possible strengths and weaknesses of all the web-based resources that you can think of. Compare your list with those of other learners.

PROJECT SPRINGBOARD

Should private schools be allowed? Should parents be banned from paying for their children to receive music or tennis lessons? Discuss your ideas and try to justify them within one or more ethical frameworks.

Project springboards

In various places in this Guide you will find *Project springboards*. These include suggestions for areas that might be developed into an Extended Project.

Icons

In the Activity and Project Springboard boxes, there are blue and green buttons with letters on them. The blue buttons indicate which of the three Functional Skills the activity helps you achieve:

 English   ICT   Mathematics.

The green buttons show which of the Personal, Learning and Thinking Skills (PLTS) the activity helps you acquire. PLTS are an essential part of the Diploma. Here is what they represent:

IE Independent enquirers   **TW** Team workers

CT Creative thinkers   **SM** Self-managers

RL Reflective learners   **EP** Effective participators

PROJECT HINT

A key aspect of your Project is that you will have to present arguments to persuade other people to your way of thinking.

COURSE REFERENCE

For a summary of commonly used ethical frameworks, see Chapter 2 of this Guide.

RESOURCE LINK

For more on SETI, visit www.seti.org

Project hints

These alert you to points that are particularly relevant to your Project (though, of course, all the material in this Guide is relevant!).

Course references

Course references direct you to relevant activities, lessons or sections elsewhere in this Guide.

Resource links

The notes headed *Resource links* guide you to additional resources relating to particular topics. You might use these in relation to particular activities or as pointers towards information sources for a project.

1 Gathering information

1.1 Questions, questions

Asking questions

One of the first things you will need to do for your Project is to research some information. To carry out research, you have to ask questions. The skill of asking the right questions underlies many areas of work; for example, journalists, scientists and historians (Figure 1.1) all ask questions. Finding the right questions to ask may be the most difficult part of your work.

Figure 1.1 Simon Schama, Clare Balding and Stephen Hawking – they ask the questions!

PROJECT HINT

The '5 W' questions provide a useful framework for analysing any source of information. Use them with the sources you consult for your Project.

When researching an event, it is useful to start with the '5 W' questions:

• *What* happened?

• *Who* were the people involved?

• *When* did it happen?

• *Where* did it happen?

• *Why* did it happen?

The answers to these questions allow you to pose many more questions, such as what were the motives of the people involved, what were the influences on them, and what were the consequences of the decisions that they made and the actions that they took.

Note that some of the answers to these questions may be **objective** facts (dates, places, names) and others **subjective** opinion (motives, influences) and that the answers depend on the sources used. Some answers may also involve **speculation** (guessing!) about past or future events.

ACTIVITY 1: FINDING ANSWERS

Practise answering the five questions listed above for a recent news item. The news item could be a sporting occasion or a celebrity event and need not be related to your Project area. Find out the answers to the '5 W' questions. What further questions would you like answered?

Researchers need to be able to produce a report on their findings. Write a brief report (a few hundred words) on your chosen news item, ensuring that you answer all the questions that you have posed.

ACTIVITY 2: FACT OR SPECULATION?

Read the following short extract from an article about killing pests. Analyse the article using the '5 W' questions and note any instances of fact, speculation or opinion.

Corpses of the dead kill the living

A cheap eco-friendly alternative to pesticides will soon be tested in Tanzania.

The African army worm (*Spodoptera exempta*) can reach plague proportions, with over 1000 caterpillars per square metre, and wipe out over 90% of a maize crop. At the moment the only cost-effective way to control it is to bombard it with pesticides, but these have obvious disadvantages: a 1990 UN report estimated that 11 million farmers in Africa suffer from pesticide poisoning each year.

A more environmentally friendly solution is to use a kind of nucleopolyhedrovirus (NPV) that infects only the army worm. Applied in large quantities it can start a massive outbreak devastating the pest. But mass-producing viruses like NPV in the quantities required to tackle army worms costs more than pesticides.

So David Grzywacz at the University of Greenwich in London is instead copying a method used in Brazil to deal with outbreaks of the velvet bean caterpillar that feeds on soya. There, workers watch for outbreaks early in the season, infect the caterpillar with a virus, then collect tonnes of dead, virus laden caterpillars. The caterpillars can be mashed up and used as a spray to tackle later outbreaks.

This is significant because farmers are already used to spraying. "The easier it is to use, the easier it will be to get them to adopt it," says Grzywacz. He hopes mass production of NPV virus in Tanzania will enable the virus to be sold to farmers for just a tenth of the price of pesticides.

James Randerson, *New Scientist*, 13 December 2003, p. 12

1.2 Sources of evidence

Publishing research work

Answering questions requires evidence. To answer questions in any Extended Project, a wide variety of sources of evidence can be used. Some of the marks for your Project will be given for the variety and quality of resources that you use to gather evidence.

One important source of evidence is researchers' own accounts of their work. Usually researchers want to communicate their work to other researchers, and sometimes to a wider audience. They may report on the work they have done by writing a paper for a research journal or by publishing a book or pamphlet.

All research areas (e.g. history, sociology, science) have their own research journals. Many of these have origins that go back many years; for example, scientific journals began to appear in the late seventeenth century. The Italian Galileo Galilei (1564–1642) described his discoveries in astronomy and mechanics early in the seventeenth century in books that he published (e.g. *The Starry Messenger and Discourses on Two New Sciences*). By the time that British scientist Isaac Newton (1642–1727) was discovering the law of gravitation, the Royal Society in London was producing its journal *Philosophical Transactions* – and it continues to do so in the present day. Today, there are thousands of research journals in many different languages. Some deal with particular topics within a research area while others cover a wider range of subjects. Many journals are published on the Internet as well as on paper.

For at least the last century, the accepted way of publishing research work has been by **peer review**. This means that the work is checked by other researchers before it is published.

Comment on a discovery may be found in other papers written at about the same time by supporters and opponents of the main characters in the story.

PEER REVIEW AND PUBLICATION

- *The researcher (or a group of researchers) writes a report on their work.*

- *They choose which journal is appropriate for their work and send their report to the editor.*

- *The journal editors (or their staff) look at the paper and decide who is best qualified to review it.*

- *Copies of the paper are sent to the chosen reviewers. They read the paper, check it for errors and comment on whether the conclusions are justified.*

- *The editor receives the comments from the reviewers and decides whether to publish the paper.*

- *Peer review is usually anonymous, so the authors of the paper do not know who reviewed it.*

- *Sometimes the editor may return the paper and ask for changes to be made before it is published; this sometimes involves passing on comments from the reviewers.*

- *A paper refused by one journal may be accepted by another.*

- *The process often takes months, but for exciting bits of research the editor may rush things through in a week or two.*

- *Sometimes, if researchers want to establish their priority in a discovery, they can send a letter or a brief summary of their work to a journal, which the editor may decide to publish without peer review.*

Contemporary magazines and newspapers may also provide commentary. Magazines such as *The Economist, Current Archaeology* and *New Scientist* provide a weekly or monthly summary of news and controversy.

A variety of sources

You will need to consult a variety of resources for your Project. Your choice of resources will depend on the type of project you are carrying out.

If you are working on a dissertation, a literature search will form a central part of your work. You will need to find out what other people have written or said about your topic, and you will probably need to research details of particular events or discoveries.

For an investigation or field study, you will need to consult textbooks and websites for background theory and information, and for details

RESOURCE LINK

Current Archaeology, New Scientist and many other such magazines can be accessed online.

of procedures (including safety regulations). You will also need to keep your own record of results and observations as you generate your own information. You will also need to look at the results of other people's work on the same topic, and at the background to that work.

Similarly, if the outcome of your Project is to be an artefact or performance, you will need information about methods and techniques and, possibly, rules and regulations (e.g. health and safety regulations or rules about the use of copyright materials). You will need to look into the context of your Project and give some background to your work.

In all cases, you will need to consult written sources such as books, journals, manuals and websites. As well as the written word, there are other sources of information. For recent events there may be audio-visual recordings of radio and TV news items or programmes, or taped interviews with key people.

Then there are artefacts. If you are making an artefact yourself, you will obviously want to study those made by others. But artefacts can be relevant to other types of project too. Banksy's graffiti could be relevant to a project looking at culture and social change, while a blackboard written on by Einstein might throw interesting light on a science project.

Finally, the place where an event took place may reveal answers to questions. Some of the places where famous people worked have been preserved (Figure 1.2). However, others have been neglected while many, of course, have been totally changed.

Figure 1.2 The church of St Lawrence, Little Stanmore, where Handel played the organ.

Some sources of evidence and information are **primary sources**. They are produced or used by the people involved in the event in question, and the accounts are written or spoken by people who were either actively involved in the event or eye-witnesses to it (Figure 1.3).

Secondary sources include biographies, books, articles and programmes about scientific topics and general histories of science, usually written after the event and by people who were not directly involved. Such sources can be very useful to the researcher, particularly to you, the learner. Here someone else has done the primary research for you.

A particular problem with relying on secondary sources for information about a historical event is that you only have the writer's interpretation of the primary evidence. It may be a surprise to some people but researchers can interpret the same evidence in a variety of ways. These viewpoints may be political so that, for example, you have the Marxist view of history or the feminist slant on discoveries. It is probably impossible to be totally objective in analysing a piece of evidence, but you must be aware of the different viewpoints of writers and commentators (Figure 1.4).

ACTIVITY 3: COMPARING SOURCES

Compare the three extracts printed below. Analyse each report by writing a few words in response to each of the '5 W' questions. Then write one or two sentences to answer the following questions.

1. Which readers are the articles aimed at?

2. What differences are there in the way the information is presented? For instance, does one report present more details about the event? Is one account more positive than the others?

Spectacular opening for Olympics

China has presented a dramatic display of fireworks, music and dancing to mark the opening of its Beijing Olympics.

Some 10,000 performers took part in the ceremony, watched on TV by an estimated one billion people, before athletes paraded around the national stadium.

Security was tight in the capital, and three US activists were arrested after holding a pro-Tibet protest. Larger rallies took place in Nepal and India.

Analysts say it is the most politicised Games since the Cold War era. The build-up to the event was dogged by worries over pollution and criticism of China's rights record.

Beijing has faced pressure to improve civil liberties – with US President George W Bush among several world leaders to express concern over a crackdown on dissidents.

But after the controversy of the run-up, the opening ceremony certainly changed the focus of attention. Some 90,000 fans packed the new national stadium – known as the Bird's Nest because of its steel lattice construction – and cheered the performers.

The choreographed show took seven years to plan. It began at eight minutes past eight on the evening of 8 August, reflecting the belief widespread in Asia that eight is a lucky number. More than three hours later, China's President Hu Jintao officially declared the Games open.

And in a theatrical finish to the day's activities, champion gymnast Li Ning was winched up to the rim of the stadium carrying the Olympic torch – the end of its journey around the world.

He used the torch to light the Olympic cauldron – in the form of another huge torch – and an explosion of fireworks ensued.

BBC News Asia-Pacific, 8 August 2008

The Olympic Opening Ceremony as it happened

11.25 pm

Figure 1.3
China's team at the
Olympics ceremony
in Beijing

At last! It's been on the go for more than three hours. Men have clapped, women have cheered, children have cried and nations have come and gone. But finally, as the last semi-dry section of shirt sticks resolutely to my back ... enter the dragon.

The China team have plumped for red on this occasion. Reminiscent of Jonathan Ross in the early 1990s, one could argue that it's an all-too-predictable outfit, but at least they're not wearing chinos or flat caps.

Crowd noise has now reached a new level, the ferocity of its roar fuelled by pent-up anticipation and national pride. For the first time tonight I feel humble; this is their celebration and we are their guests. OK, so it's gone on a bit, but you can't deny it's been a success.

Arrangements are made for the torch-lighting ceremony. We really are about to begin...

Times Online, 8 August 2008

Television review: Olympic Opening Ceremony, BBC1

Confronted with 2,008 drummers beating a holy tattoo of light and sound, Huw Edwards knew he had to come up with something. He hadn't been sent to the Beijing Olympic Opening Ceremony just to look sweaty. As the drummers formed a staggering numerical display – like the LED train timetables at Euston, but made entirely of people – Edwards reached deep into the bran-tub of his brain. "That," he said, "was quite something."

Live commentary is a tough game, and over the course of the ceremony the BBC team found its stride, providing a good flow of translation, explanation and downright exultation at the alien beauty of it all – though there were a few goofs to cherish. The opening moments of the games – with fire fizzing round the rim of the stadium – was not the right time to ask former athletes to put the event in political context. (Come to think of it, is there ever a right time?)

*Figure 1.4
Commentators at
a sport event*

And Sue Barker, why oh why? As a magical clock in computer generated imagery ticked off the seconds to the new Olympiad, did you really have to say: "Huw, this is a countdown Carol Vorderman would be more than impressed by."

Ah, cosy British parochialism, we clasp you like a comfort blanket in the face of the might of China's superlative opening ceremony. However will our Morris dancers compete? Even when arranged in the formation of a huge pork pie?

After the Olympic flame was lit with an aerial routine straight out of Raymond Briggs, but faster ("We're sprinting in the air") a BBC announcer cheerily told us that due to the length, breadth and scale of the Olympic opening ceremony, there was no time for the scheduled episode of Flog It. Britain suddenly felt like a very small country.

Hermione Eyre, *The Independent,* 10 August 2008

PROJECT SPRINGBOARD

1. Look at the arts review or sports section in a recent issue of a national newspaper. What topics are covered? Choose one topic and summarise the content of the article. Does it answer the basic '5 W' questions? What is the attitude of the author(s)?

2. Most researchers are in favour of peer review but some oppose it. Discuss the advantages and disadvantages of peer review.

3. In what ways do you think the Internet might affect the communication of research work?

1.3 Researching information

At this stage you might have an opportunity to visit an academic library, either in a university or as part of an organisation (such as the Courtauld Institute or the Wellcome Trust) specialising in a particular subject. During your visit, notice how publications are arranged and catalogued. Have a look at some academic journals and see how papers are set out, with headings, references and acknowledgments. If possible, compare the styles of more recent journals with some from earlier centuries. Talk to the library staff and note the name of anyone who might be able to help you use the library on a future occasion.

1.4 Using web resources

Strengths and weaknesses of web resources

In the course of your Project, you will almost certainly want to make use of the vast resources available via the Internet (Figure 1.5). Just as you would with any source, it is important to think critically about what you read on the Internet. You cannot assume that what you are reading is objective, unbiased fact.

ACTIVITY 4: STRENGTHS AND WEAKNESSES OF WEB RESOURCES

List the possible strengths and weaknesses of all the web-based resources that you can think of. Compare your list with those of other learners.

Evaluating web resources

When you are browsing the web to help your research, you should be asking yourself questions both in order to understand what you read and also to evaluate reliability and validity.

The '5 W' questions

Earlier you encountered the '5 W' questions: *what, who, when, where* and *why*. These can be applied to the material you find on the web. When doing web research, key questions to ask include:

• What is this site telling me?

• Who put this material on the web?

• When was this information placed here? (Is it still up to date?)

• Where is the information placed? (What site does it belong to?)

• Why has this information been placed on the web? (Is it there merely to inform, or is it meant to convince me of a particular point of view?)

Figure 1.5
Using the Internet.

Primary or secondary?

You have already learned about the importance of distinguishing between primary and secondary sources. This is especially significant when reading material published on the Internet, since much of it is not factual but represents a personal point of view, or speculation. The key questions here are:

• Is this material a primary or secondary source?

• Is the material fact, subjective opinion or speculation?

Reliability

Establishing the reliability of web material is not easy, but questions that can be asked include:

• How much authority does the author have? (e.g. are they a recognised expert, a student or an interested amateur?)

• Is the site where the work is published a reputable source? (e.g. does it have a reputation for impartiality? Has the research been peer reviewed?)

• Is the process by which the information was obtained rigorous? (e.g. is it based on controlled testing? Was the sample used sufficiently large and unbiased?)

ACTIVITY 5: EVALUATING WEB RESOURCES   iE

Choose a website with information relevant to your Project and carry out an evaluation using the questions listed above.

2 Thinking skills

2.1 Right and wrong

An important part of your project work will involve careful thinking. You may need to consider what is the right or wrong course of action for you to take in a particular situation, or to evaluate actions taken by others.

What is right and what is wrong?

Ethics is an intellectual discipline, just as subjects like mathematics, music, history and science are. Each of these intellectual disciplines has its own ways of working. By and large, the ways of working that are appropriate to one discipline can't simply be transferred to another. Thus, the laws of mathematics can help us to prove that the number of prime numbers is infinite and that the square root of two is irrational, but they can't help us to decide whether Beethoven's Ninth is his greatest symphony. And the scientific way of working that helps us to determine the factors that affect the boiling point of water (pressure and impurities in the water) doesn't really help us to understand why Harold lost the Battle of Hastings.

The discipline of **ethics** is all about deciding what is morally right and what is morally wrong, and why. **Morals** are beliefs about whether things are right or wrong. For example, is it right or wrong to eat meat, to have sex before you are 16, or to sometimes tell lies? Ethics has its own ways of working. Fortunately, while some of us are hopeless at mathematics and others of us are tone deaf or have no interest in history, just about all of us spend quite a bit of our time reasoning ethically. So you almost certainly already have quite a bit of knowledge to help you understand ethics.

Ethical questions are particularly prevalent in science. For example, is it acceptable to use animals in medical experiments, to undertake human reproductive cloning or to develop nuclear bombs? However, the reasoning that is used to answer such questions follows the same rules and procedures as the reasoning to answer any ethical question. We will start therefore with an apparently simple everyday question: "Why is it wrong to steal?" (Figure 2.1).

Figure 2.1
Stealing is generally regarded as wrong.

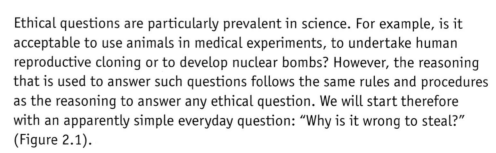

ACTIVITY 6: WHAT IS WRONG WITH STEALING?

In pairs or small groups, spend five minutes thinking of as many possible different reasons why it might be wrong to steal. At this stage, don't start arguing about whether each reason is valid or not – just generate a number of possible reasons and write them down.

ACTIVITY 7: EXPLORING YOUR REASONS

After spending five minutes or so on Activity 6, start trying to explore the reasons a bit further. Think of their implications. For example, suppose one of your reasons for believing that stealing is wrong is that in the absence of this widely held view people would be very afraid that their property would be forcibly taken from them. One implication is that we might expect people with lots of personal property to feel more strongly that stealing is wrong than people with little personal property. Do you think this is the case?

Thinking carefully, as in Activity 7, should help you to refine your reasons so that, even if you don't believe all of them, you can mount an intellectual defence of each of them. Of course, if you don't believe one of the reasons given, in your pair or group work, try arguing with whoever proposed it to see if you can validly change their mind. At the same time, you need to be open to the possibility that they are right and that you will have to change your mind.

ACTIVITY 8: CATEGORISING REASONS

Try to put your reasons from Activities 6 and 7 into categories. For example, if you believe that the reason why it is wrong to steal is that having this prohibition is, overall, the best policy for all members of society, this is an example of utilitarian thinking.

We shall have more to say about **utilitarianism** in the next lesson, but it's enough to say that utilitarians think that things are right in the world if they maximise the amount of happiness, and wrong if they lead to more unhappiness. So a utilitarian would favour the law 'Don't steal' if, overall, this led to greater happiness than allowing a free-for-all.

Another category – though one that fewer people use nowadays than in the past – is that of **divine command**. If you feel that stealing is wrong, because it breaks one of the Ten Commandments or is forbidden in the Qur'an, for example, then you presumably have a strong religious faith and believe that the scriptures of your faith help you decide what is right and what is wrong.

Another category might be that people have certain rights, and these include the right to retain one's property. In everyday language, we might say that it isn't fair to steal from someone; but try thinking about whether it makes a difference how the person acquired that which someone else wants to steal. For example, is stealing from someone who has worked hard to acquire property worse than stealing from someone who has won it on the lottery or inherited it from their parents?

ACTIVITY 9: WHAT IS THEFT?

Explore precisely what is meant by theft. For example, suppose I have a girlfriend/boyfriend and you don't and you attempt to entice my girlfriend/boyfriend away from me. Is this theft? If you think it is, explain why. If you think it isn't, explain why it isn't. Is it theft when a government requires its citizens to pay taxes? And what about the fact that tax rates are nearly always higher for people with greater incomes. Is this stealing? Are there any distinctions that can be drawn between income tax and inheritance tax? Quickly jot down your ideas and then spend about 10 minutes discussing them with other learners.

PROJECT SPRINGBOARD

1. Find out a bit about the land distribution programme in Zimbabwe, as instituted by Robert Mugabe's government. Discuss whether this is an example of theft and therefore unethical, or an example of reducing indefensible inequalities and so ethical.

2. Consider why theft seems to be almost universal in human societies even though nearly everyone thinks it is wrong.

2.2 Introducing ethical frameworks

Ethical frameworks

There is no one universally agreed way of deciding what is right and what is wrong. Instead there are a number of **ethical frameworks** that can be used. Quite often the same answers to ethical questions are reached whichever framework is used, but sometimes the different frameworks generate very different answers. Most people don't fully appreciate the reasons why they hold the ethical views that they do. Appreciating the range of different ethical frameworks should help you sharpen your ethical thinking and allow you to evaluate ethical arguments used by others.

What are the consequences?

The simplest approach to deciding whether an action would be right or wrong is to look at what its consequences would be. No one supposes that we can ignore the consequences of an action before deciding whether or not it is right. The deeper question is whether that is all that we need to do. Are there certain actions – such as telling the truth – that are morally required whatever their consequences? Are there other actions – such as betraying confidences – that are wrong whatever their consequences?

Those who believe that consequences alone are sufficient to let a person decide the rightness or otherwise of a course of action are called **consequentialists**. The most widespread form of consequentialism is known as **utilitarianism**. Utilitarianism itself takes various forms, but it begins with the assumption that most actions lead to pleasure and/or suffering. In a situation in which there are alternative courses of action, the right action is the one which leads to the greatest net increase in pleasure.

Consider the question as to whether or not we should tell the truth. A utilitarian would hesitate to provide an unqualified 'yes' as a universal answer. Utilitarians have no moral absolutes beyond the maximisation of pleasure principle. It would be necessary for a utilitarian to look in some detail at particular cases and see in each of them whether telling the truth would indeed lead to the greatest net increase in pleasure.

ACTIVITY 10: A UTILITARIAN APPROACH CT

Jot down a list of the sort of information that a utilitarian would need in order to decide whether factory farming should be permitted.

Divine command

People with a religious faith or who were brought up in a religious family often attach great significance to the teachings of their religion in ethical matters. Right conduct is seen as fulfilling what is required by **divine command**. In some religious traditions, what is of paramount importance is what is contained in sacred scriptures; in other religious traditions, such writings are interpreted to the community by a specialised group of people, such as priests.

The scriptures of the world's great religions (Figure 2.2) have a great deal to say about such human matters as ownership, warfare, sexuality, hospitality, honesty and selfishness. However, they have rather less to say about science. Nevertheless, people with a strong religious faith often have very firm views about ethical issues in science, such as abortion, the use of animals in medical experiments and genetic engineering.

Figure 2.2 Sacred scriptures contain guidance on human behaviour.

ACTIVITY 11: CONSIDERING FAITH-BASED VIEWS

What consideration should be given to the ethical views of those with a strong religious faith? Discuss your opinions. Try to think of examples of situations where religious views are either taken into account or ignored.

2.3 Further ethical frameworks

Rights and duties

A further ethical framework starts from the notion of **rights**. Not all philosophers accept that rights exist, but the notion of rights has been of great political value. They are enshrined in a number of constitutions. For example, the Constitution of the USA (Figure 2.3) holds the rights of life, liberty and the pursuit of happiness to be inalienable. More recently, rights have been extended to children in the 1989 United Nations Convention on the Rights of the Child, while some argue that animals (non-human animals) have certain rights too.

*Figure 2.3
The Constitution of
the USA*

Rights are accompanied by **duties**, but the relationship between rights and duties is often misunderstood. It is typically supposed that if you have rights, then you also have duties – as in the political slogan that rights need to be accompanied by responsibilities. To see the logical error in this, consider a newborn baby (Figure 2.4). If ever a creature had rights, it is surely a newborn baby. Presumably a baby has the right to be fed, kept warm, protected and loved. But what duties does a baby have? Surely none. A newborn baby is simply too young to have duties, and it is not yet responsible for its actions. However, others have duties to it – namely, to feed it, keep it warm, protect it and love it. Normally such duties are fulfilled by the child's parent(s), but if neither parent is able to undertake these duties, for whatever reason, the duties pass to others, for example, other relatives, adoptive parents or social services. In general, if A has a right, there is a B who has a duty to ensure that A's rights are met.

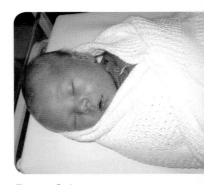

Figure 2.4
A newborn baby

One of the rights that we normally presume people have is the right to make their own decisions about their lives. We believe that we should respect people's **autonomy** (their right to govern themselves). In medicine, for example, we are less likely than thirty years ago to assume that we should do what a doctor tells us simply because a doctor has told us to do it. We expect to be told about the implications of any possible alternative courses of action and then to give our informed consent to one of them.

ACTIVITY 12: WHAT RIGHTS DO YOU HAVE? CT

Write down a list of rights that you believe you have now, and a second list of additional rights that you expect to have within a few years' time.

Virtue ethics

A rather different approach to the whole issue of ethics is provided by **virtue ethics**. Instead of starting from particular actions and trying to decide whether they maximise the amount of happiness in the world, are divinely forbidden or infringe someone's rights, virtue ethics focuses on the characteristics of good people. For example, think about a good teacher. What characteristics might you expect them to have? You might want them to know their subject, to treat all students fairly, to be able to maintain order in the classroom, to maximise your chances of doing well in any examinations, to be able to communicate clearly, to have a sense of humour, and so on. Some of these are skills – for example, the ability to maintain order – but some are personality traits that we call virtues – notably treating all students fairly, rather than, for example, favouring males, Asians, high-attaining students or Chelsea supporters.

ACTIVITY 13: VIRTUES

Spend about five minutes discussing the following:

• What characteristics might you hope to find in a lifelong partner? Which of these are virtues?

• Suppose you have to spend a week in hospital. What characteristics might you hope to find in the nursing staff? Which of these are virtues?

Absolutism and relativism

A final point to consider is whether ethical judgements are absolute or relative. Both these words are used in a variety of ways, but **absolutism** presumes the existence of an objective reason for a statement. So, someone might argue that it is absolutely wrong to torture people because such behaviour is forbidden in scripture, is inherently disrespectful to people, contravenes their rights or always leads to unhappiness. On the other hand, a position that derives from **relativism** may be just as much against torturing people but argue that torture is wrong because we decide it is, rather than for any other absolute reason.

Many people don't like the idea of relativism in ethics, realising that it means that there are no absolute rights or wrongs. In different circumstances (including in different places and at different times), relativists may come up with a different list of what is right and what is wrong.

Relativists respond to such accusations in various ways. Firstly, they point to the lessons of history. In the past, for example, slavery was routinely used in many countries. Does that mean that such people were necessarily bad in the way that someone who kept slaves in Surrey would be today? Or consider votes for women. At one point no country had such a thing. Nowadays practically every democracy does. The lesson of history is that what is right and what is wrong depends, at least to some extent, on the circumstances.

Secondly, relativists ask where absolute knowledge about ethics comes from. As we saw earlier, some people believe it has divine authority. But many people argue that what is right and what is wrong is worked out in debate between people. In this view, ethics is all about learning how to get on sufficiently adequately with your neighbour so that society can function reasonably well.

ACTIVITY 14: ABSOLUTISM OR RELATIVISM?

Do you believe in absolutism or relativism? Defend your answer.

PROJECT SPRINGBOARD

Using two of the ethical frameworks that you have studied, discuss whether or not stealing is wrong. (About 400 words should be ample for a written answer.)

2.4 Dealing with inequality

Distributive justice

One important ethical consideration is justice. There are several sorts of justice of which perhaps the most important for ethics is **distributive justice**. This means that scarce resources should be allocated among people in a way that is fair. For example, your chances of getting a fair trial should not depend on how much money you have. This is the basis of legal aid. If you have little money, the State pays someone to represent you legally. Of course, things are never as straightforward as this, and if you are wealthy, you will almost certainly be able to obtain better legal representation.

The following extract describes two '**thought experiments**' on this theme. The intended reader is an academic in the USA.

The Shallow Pond

The path from the library at your university to the humanities lecture hall passes a shallow ornamental pond. On your way to give a lecture, you notice that a small child has fallen in and is in danger of drowning. If you wade in and pull the child out, it will mean getting your clothes muddy and either cancelling the lecture or delaying it until you can find something clean and dry to wear. If you pass by the child, then, while you'll give your lecture on time, the child will die straightaway. You pass by and, as expected, the child dies.

The Envelope

In your mailbox, there's something from [the US Committee for] UNICEF. After reading it through, you correctly believe that, unless you soon send in a cheque for $100, then, instead of each living many more years, over thirty more children will die soon. But, you throw the material in your trash basket, including the convenient return envelope provided, you send nothing, and, instead of living many more years, over thirty more children die sooner than would have had you sent in the requested $100.

Unger, P., *Living High & Letting Die: Our Illusion of Innocence* (Oxford University Press, 1996), p. 9

ACTIVITY 15: BEHAVING BADLY?

What would you think of someone who behaved as the academic did in 'The Shallow Pond' situation? What would you think of someone who behaved as the person did in 'The Envelope' situation? If you feel that one of these two people has behaved morally worse than the other, why do you feel this way? Do you think you should feel this way? Talk to other learners and compare your views with theirs.

ACTIVITY 16: LIFE EXPECTANCY

The following extract is on the same general theme of distributive justice. Read it and study the graph, and then discuss whether you think it is acceptable that there are considerable health inequalities in England and Wales.

Gap between classes in life expectancy is widening

Healthcare providers, local authorities, schools, employers, and the voluntary sector need to work together more closely to narrow the gap in health differences between different parts of the country and between different social groups, the health secretary said last week. (See Figure 2.5.)

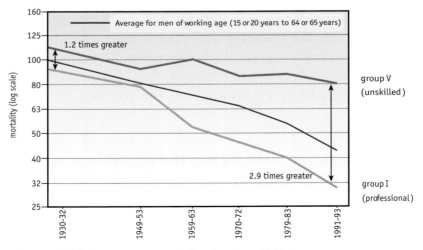

Figure 2.5 Life expectancy in England and Wales

Despite some improvements, the health gap between the top and bottom classes of the social scale remains large and is getting wider in some areas. Between 1930 and 1990 the gap between mortality among professional men and that among men in unskilled manual jobs increased almost two and half times. The difference can mean an extra 10 or more years of life for wealthier people.

In his document the health secretary, John Reid, sets out a three year plan to cut inequalities in health. He also spells out the actions that are needed to achieve the 2010 targets of reducing infant mortality by 10% across social groups and raising by 10% life expectancy in the most disadvantaged areas of the country, compared with the population as a whole.

"For too long we have been prepared to tolerate glaring differences in health between different parts of our country and different groups within it. Why should we accept that a man born in Manchester can expect to live, on average, ten years less than one born in Dorset and that a woman in Manchester is likely to live seven years less than a woman born in Somerset? And why should we accept that manual workers and some ethnic minorities appear condemned to suffer worse health?"

Zosia Kmietowicz, *British Medical Journal* 327 (2003), p. 68

PROJECT SPRINGBOARD

Should private schools be allowed? Should parents be banned from paying for their children to receive music or tennis lessons? Discuss your ideas and try to justify them within one or more ethical frameworks.

2.5 Reasons and points of view

Be reasonable

In your Project, you will be expected to develop your own point of view on issues relating to your work, and to defend that point of view.

There are many questions which cannot be settled simply by finding out the relevant facts. These are questions which concern fundamental ideas – questions about what is truly real and what we can really know. On questions like these, different people form different **points of view**.

PROJECT HINT

A key aspect of your Project is that you will have to present arguments to persuade other people to your way of thinking.

Some people, for example, take the point of view that the physical world is all that there is (a point of view known as **materialism**). Others take the point of view that there is a god beyond the universe (a point of view known as **theism**).

One of the sad aspects of the history of ideas is that these differences have often led to one group of people imposing their point of view on others, often using the threat of violence to do so. A better way to deal with differences of viewpoint is to use evidence, reason and argument to try to persuade other people of your point of view. You will find yourself using arguments at various points in your Project.

- If you are writing a dissertation, you will have to advance arguments to support your point of view, and also consider and reply to counter-arguments.

- If you are conducting an investigation or field study, you will have to use arguments to show why your interpretation of the data is better than alternative interpretations.

- If you are creating an artefact, you will have to create arguments to justify the key design decisions you have made. This will involve giving reasons in favour of one approach over another.

- If you are putting on a performance, arguments will probably happen about how best to stage your performance.

PROJECT HINT

The skill of laying out arguments is an important one for your Project. It will help you to present your own arguments clearly, and to analyse those put forward by other people.

The key point is that arguments need not be unpleasant quarrels – they can be a helpful part of the process of searching for the truth, or finding your way towards better, more creative solutions to problems. The key is to argue clearly, logically and respectfully – recognising that other people have viewpoints which may also be reasonable, even if you disagree with them.

So what is an argument? An argument is a piece of reasoning used to persuade someone to accept a **proposition** (a statement of a point of view) by showing how it follows logically as a **conclusion** from reasonable assumptions. These assumptions are called the **premises** of the argument.

You can learn a lot about how arguments work by reading some, then working out how they are structured. It is a good first step, when reading an argument, to ask yourself what the argument is seeking to prove (what the conclusion is) and what premises it begins from. These points will help in laying out the structure of someone's reasoning:

- Useful clues in identifying the conclusion of an argument are phrases such as "I take the view that…", "Therefore …", or "It follows that…".

- The conclusion is not necessarily the last sentence in the argument.

Often, the conclusion is stated at the start of the argument or even midway through.

• The author may present several different arguments for the same point of view. It is helpful to list each of the arguments separately and consider each on its own merits.

• People often argue for several different conclusions at once. You will have to think carefully to decide on the main point the person is seeking to establish.

ACTIVITY 17: LAYING OUT ARGUMENTS

The arguments below all refer to the existence or otherwise of 'aliens' (Figure 2.6). For each argument, identify the point of view which the author is seeking to support (the conclusion of the argument) and the reasons which are given to support it (the premises). Present your summary in a table with two columns, headed 'premises' and 'conclusion', and one numbered row for each of the arguments. Write a sentence or two under each heading. Laying out the arguments in this way shows, in each case, how the premises lead to the conclusion.

Argument 1

There must be life on other planets. The Universe is such a big place.

Argument 2

If there are aliens, they would have visited us by now. So there probably aren't any.

Argument 3

For complex life forms to evolve takes incredible delicately balanced conditions. It therefore seems unlikely that alien life forms exist. After all, we only know that the right conditions exist on Earth.

Figure 2.6 Aliens.

Argument 4

I think that it all depends on how you define life. Simple organisms could well have evolved in many places in the universe; but the existence of complex life forms is much less likely.

Argument 5

If there are aliens, they would never be able to find us in such a big universe. Our best chance of finding them is by searching for radio messages.

Argument 6

It seems likely that we will, eventually, find out that life is not unique to Earth. If it was true that the Earth was the centre of the universe, it would be reasonable to assume that life was unique to Earth. But science has shown us that the Earth is not the centre of the universe. This conclusion is supported by the fact that we are discovering more and more planets which could contain life.

Valid and invalid reasons

Once you have identified the reasons someone gives for their point of view, you should evaluate whether they are good reasons. The terms 'valid' and 'invalid' are useful here.

When reasons support a point of view, we call them **valid**. Say, for example, that your point of view is that aliens might well exist, and your reason is that anything is possible in a large enough universe. This would be a valid reason for believing that aliens might exist, since if anything is possible, then aliens are possible. The reason you have given provides support for your point of view.

It is quite common for people to form points of view without valid supporting reasons. They might simply believe in aliens as a matter of faith. Or they might think that they have reasons, but they are not in fact valid. Consider someone who believes that aliens exist because they can't bear the thought that we are alone in the universe. In other words, they believe in aliens as a result of wishful thinking. This is not a valid reason, since the fact that someone wants a belief to be true does not make it likely to be true. In this case, we would say that their reasons are **invalid**. A good tip for improving the strength of your Project is to check that whenever you advance a point of view on a particular question it is backed up by valid lines of argument.

> **PROJECT HINT**
>
> In your Project, look for examples of valid and invalid reasons used in arguments. Spotting an invalid reason will enable you to respond to an argument against your own point of view. When putting forward an argument to support your own viewpoint, think carefully about your reasons and make sure they are valid.

Figure 2.7 The Arecibo radio telescope which is used in SETI

PROJECT SPRINGBOARD

There are many good and – at present – unanswered scientific questions about the possible or probable existence of extraterrestrial life. But there are also philosophical questions about the purpose of the quest and its implications for our concept of human beings and their place in the universe.

Read the following extract from an interview with Paul Davies and discuss your views about the Search for Extraterrestrial Intelligence (SETI) project (Figure 2.7). (Paul Davies is a professor of physics with a particular interest in the relationships between science and religion.) Why does Davies think SETI is a religious enterprise? In your view, is he right about this? Should SETI be seen as science, pseudoscience, a philosophy or a religion?

> Frank Drake, the grandfather of SETI, once said that the search for intelligent life elsewhere in the universe is really a search for ourselves. It is a search for who we are and what our place is in the great scheme of things. Whether SETI succeeds or not, it fosters interesting conversations. Like the world's great religions, it asks: What is a human being? What is intelligence? What kind of place is the universe? Different people derive comfort from different answers. Some like to think that we are in splendid isolation, while others – and I'm in this category – like to think we live in a bio-friendly universe in which the emergence of life and mind – consciousness – is built into the scheme of things in a deep way. Interestingly, people who engage in SETI seem to be atheists or even militant atheists. Jill Tarter, director of the Center for SETI Research, has been very outspoken against religion, and yet I see SETI's quest as fundamentally religious.

Paul Davies, 'The next philosophy' (online interview) www.niburu.nl

PROJECT HINT

An aspect of SETI might make an interesting topic for your Project.

2.6 Reasons and objections

Reasons, objections and replies

It is very rare indeed for a theory to be accepted by everyone. In almost all debates, there are reasons for and against a given point of view. During the course of your work on your Project, you will come up against the fact that not everyone thinks like you do – not everyone shares your point of view. If you are going to build a case for your particular point of view, you will need to identify and respond to the **objections** which can be raised against it.

ACTIVITY 18: REASONS, OBJECTIONS AND REPLIES

The following extract is taken from an article by Mick Hume in *The Times*. Read it and write a series of bullet points that summarise:

- the author's point of view

- the reasons he gives

- the objections he considers to his point of view

- the answers he gives to those objections.

RESOURCE LINK

For the full text of this article, visit www.timesonline. co.uk/ type 'a grisly theatre of death' in the search engine and hit return on the keyboard. The first result will be this article.

> *A grisly theatre of death – not exactly an advertisement for a dignified end*

Dr Anne Turner, a 66-year-old retired GP suffering from progressive supranuclear palsy, went to Switzerland to kill herself with the help of Dignitas, a euthanasia clinic. Her adult children drank champagne with her, then watched as she died from a cocktail of barbiturates. ...

Campaigners argue that people should have choice and the right to die. In fact, everybody already has the 'freedom' to kill themselves and no law could stop a determined suicide. Somebody like Dr Turner, a medical professional in the early stages of degenerative disease, also had the knowledge and ability to do it. Instead, she chose to stage a grisly travelling theatre of death for the world media.

When personal tragedy is politicised in this way, it raises bigger questions about what attitude we as a society should take to life and death. Individuals may fear the future and see their situation as hopeless. But that is no reason for the rest of us to sanction their suicide wish in culture and law, in effect to say to the desperate person on the ledge: "We feel your pain — go ahead and jump."

The Dignitas clinic takes that attitude to its logical conclusion by helping to kill people such as a British couple who were depressed but not terminally ill. After all, once you claim assisted suicide as a human right, how do you deny it to anybody?

Like Dr Turner, I think of myself as a humanist. I have no truck with the religious 'pro-life' lobby and support legalised abortion just as I oppose legalised euthanasia. I hope that compassionate doctors will continue to make the end as painless as possible, as they have always done. But I also think that our society should make clear that we do not want to assist suicide or endorse euthanasia; that the law should not treat death as simply a lifestyle choice; that there must be more to human dignity than dying quietly at home.

Mick Hume, *The Times*, 27 January 2006

Objecting to yourself

We are all very much inclined to believe that our beliefs are correct. Having confidence in your convictions is very proper; yet, at the same time, we cannot neglect the possibility that what seems to us to be true might actually be false. In other words, forming a reasonable point of view means considering objections to your viewpoint.

It is much easier to think of objections to other people's point of view than it is to see objections to your own. It takes a deliberate effort of thought to ask, "if I was arguing against what I actually believe, what would I say?" Many people are content to form their opinions and perhaps find some supporting reasons. It is rarer to find someone who thinks seriously about the **counter-arguments** to their viewpoint. But, if you are going to form a really strong argument for your viewpoint, it is important to identify objections and to work out how you can respond to them.

ACTIVITY 19: OBJECTING TO YOURSELF

Consider the issue of voluntary euthanasia which Mick Hume discusses. What is your own point of view on this issue? What reasons would you give to support your viewpoint? What objections are there to your view? How would you respond to these objections? Write a few sentences on each of these questions.

PROJECT HINT

Taking a controversial issue, such as euthanasia, is a good way of giving focus to your Project. Also, because the issue is controversial, it means that there will be a range of different viewpoints which you can research, before deciding what point of view you wish to support.

PROJECT HINT

In your Project, you can strengthen your argument in favour of your point of view by identifying some objections and responding to them.

2.7 Analysing the language of arguments

Minding your language

One thing which you will be expected to do in your Project is to **analyse** the ideas you are working with. **Analysis** means exploring the meaning of the key ideas in your Project. This is important because it will help to generate new ideas which you can develop in your work and also because it will help you to achieve a deeper level of understanding.

Suppose, for example, that you are thinking about doing a project on the relationship between war and religion. Here are some of the central ideas you might want to analyse:

• What do we mean by the word 'God'?

• Do different people mean the same thing when they use the word 'God'?

• Does everyone have their own meaning for the word 'God'?

• What does it mean to truly believe in God?

• Is faith in God a virtue?

• How are faith, doubt and certainty related? (Is doubt the opposite of faith? Does faith imply certainty?)

ACTIVITY 20: ANALYSING THE MEANING OF RELIGIOUS TERMS

Discuss the meaning, or meanings, which can be attached to the words 'God', 'faith', 'belief', 'doubt' and 'certainty'. Use the questions above as a guide. Remember that religious belief is a very personal matter for many people, so keep your comments focused on the question of trying to clarify exactly what the people you are discussing with mean when they use the word.

PROJECT HINT

In the Introduction section of your Project, you need to identify and define key words and phrases. Use these guidelines to help you do so.

There are a number of things you can do to help analyse key words in your Project.

Examples

Giving examples is a helpful first step towards working out a definition for a word. It is particularly worthwhile since a single word often has more than one meaning. It is easy to forget this and look for 'the' definition. By thinking of a few examples of the way in which the word is used, you can become aware of the different meanings it can have.

Contrasts

The meaning of a word often becomes clearer when it is contrasted with other words. For example, when thinking about the meaning of a word like 'theory', we might want to contrast it with words like 'fact', and compare it with similar words, such as '**hypothesis**' or 'law'.

Checking the dictionary definition

Using a dictionary (Figure 2.8) can be a helpful step in thinking clearly about concepts. Dictionaries record how words are actually used and they often indicate when the word has more than one meaning. Bear in mind, though, that many words cannot be given simple definitions. This is particularly true when dealing with philosophical and ethical concepts, such as right and wrong, truth and falsity, and life and death. A dictionary definition can be a helpful place to start when trying to explain what a word means, but it does not remove the need for some hard thinking of your own.

Figure 2.8 Use a dictionary to help you think about key words in an argument.

> ## ACTIVITY 21: MIND MAPS
>
> Read the definition of the 'mind map' in the glossary and search the Internet for examples of mind maps and how they work.

Mind maps

Once you have found a number of different meanings for a word, or found contrasting words, it is useful to think about the relationships between them. A mind map is a good visual tool for laying out these relationships.

Reason and emotion

The point of an argument is to provide valid reasons for a point of view. This means using the skills of logical reasoning and paying careful attention to use words clearly and precisely in explaining your viewpoint. However, in reality, we are all prone to using language emotionally, and this can be particularly powerful in the course of an argument. Certainly someone who is good at using language to stir up feelings will be more likely to persuade others of their point of view (Figure 2.9).

However, there is a big difference between being swayed by the emotional appeal of a speaker's words and being rationally convinced of the logic of their case. It is not wrong to present your viewpoint in ways which make it sound appealing, but it is worthwhile, when analysing other people's arguments, checking to see whether they are carrying you towards their conclusion by relying on logic – or by emotional appeal. The danger is that

Figure 2.9 Emotive language can be used to stir up feelings.

you might find you are being skilfully manipulated and your critical thinking faculties are being lulled into inactivity.

ACTIVITY 22: LANGUAGE AND THE SETI DEBATE

Consider the way that language is used in the argument below. Identify key terms which are vague and need to be defined clearly. Using examples, contrasts and a dictionary, write a paragraph for each one, giving a clear definition. Think too about the way in which the argument uses emotive language. What words are being used to stir up your feelings? Does the argument seem persuasive because of its logical validity, or is it relying too much on an appeal to emotion? Write a paragraph to sum up your thoughts.

RESOURCE LINK

For more on SETI, visit www.seti.org

"There has to be someone out there. It is such a big universe. How can anyone believe that life exists only here on Earth? That's such an arrogant thing to think. It is just as stupid as believing that the Earth is the centre of the universe. There must be millions of other stars with planets which can support life. Surely intelligent life will have evolved on at least one of them."

ACTIVITY 23: ANALYSING KEY TERMS

One way to discuss the reliability of sources is to use the categories of fact, subjective opinion and speculation.

Write a paragraph about the meaning of each of these terms. You may like to refer to a dictionary definition. Include examples of how each term is used and a comparison of the meaning of each with the other two.

THINKING SKILLS SUMMARY

Here is a framework for thinking about issues relating to your Project. It will be especially relevant in the Discussion/Development/Analysis sections of your work.

Start by explaining clearly and precisely your own viewpoint

This involves trying to define precisely the key terms in the topic you are considering (using a dictionary, examples and contrasts). It also means 'locating' where you stand in a debate. There will be positions with which you agree, and others that you are opposed to.

Support your point of view by giving reasons

Ideally, a point of view should be backed up by supporting arguments. The focus of your reasoning should be on logical arguments, not appeals to feeling. Supporting evidence is vital, especially if you are trying to build a case in favour of a particular **hypothesis**.

Identify objections/alternative interpretations to your viewpoint

Even though you hold a particular viewpoint, much can be gained by trying to see why other people think differently.

Reply to these objections/alternative interpretations

Being able to support an argument both with logical reasons and with answers to objections/alternative views is a tremendously valuable skill – not only when discussing issues related to your Project, but in any area of work or life where debatable questions arise.

The strongest projects are those in which these thinking skills are used throughout, both when writing about particular topics and when developing ideas through dialogue with other learners or your teacher/tutor.

3 Organisation

3.1 Identifying a project topic or research question

Getting it into focus

When you begin your Project, it is important to spend time thinking about your objectives. Strong projects have clear, well-defined, achievable objectives.

In almost all cases, your Project will work best if you choose a question to research, or set yourself a design brief to work towards. Questions are valuable since all projects have to include some research, and it is easier to research if you have a clear question in mind that you are trying to answer.

Strong dissertations are those in which there is a research question which can be addressed by means of secondary research, accompanied by logical arguments and the use of evidence to build a case for your own answer to the research question.

If you are working on an investigation or field study, the focus of your Project should be on a particular hypothesis which you are able to test.

If you decide to create an artefact, you can achieve focused objectives by choosing to work on a **brief** or **commission** – a specific design task assigned by a client. This does not mean that you have to have a real client that you are working for – an imaginary client will do.

Even if you are carrying out a performance, you can still have a question in mind which your performance is designed to explore. For example, you might set out to explore a question such as "What should we be doing about climate change?", and create a performance piece to explore your point of view.

Topics

As well as a research question or brief, well-focused projects usually have a central topic. When you are thinking about your choice of project objective, it makes sense to select a topic first of all, then think about more specific, focused questions or design briefs from within that topic area. The topic can be quite general – like 'time', 'animal rights', 'fear', 'love' or 'healthy living'.

In a good project, the central topic may be examined from a number of different perspectives. It makes sense to choose a topic which you can study

> **PROJECT HINT**
>
> The narrower your focus is, the easier to research and build your Project.

using skills and knowledge drawn from a range of different subject areas which you already know about. Suppose that you are a Design student, who is also studying Psychology. Why not pick a topic – such as the influence of advertising – which can combine these two approaches?

ACTIVITY 24: CHOOSING TOPICS **CT**

Generate a list of topic areas which would form good starting points for project work. Bear in mind that it helps if you already have some knowledge about these topic areas, based on the other subjects you are studying. Think about a list of questions or design briefs which you could choose from within one of these topic areas.

The project proposal

Once you have some idea about the topic area you will explore in your Project, and have thought about the choice of research question or design brief, you will need to write a project proposal.

Do not rush this important stage of your Project. A good project proposal is a cornerstone to a successful project. It is much better to spend more time at the start, clarifying and refining your ideas, than to jump in and find that your objectives are unrealistic, vague or simply not that personally enjoyable.

When giving your reasons for choosing the project, think about this at both a personal and a social level. Your personal reasons may relate to the intrinsic interest of your topic, but try to explain *why* it is interesting. It isn't particularly impressive to simply say "I am interested in....". If you have chosen a topic because of how it links to your other subjects, or to what you plan to do in the future, talk about this. Also, explain why the topic you are working on matters to society in general. Why is it important? What difference will the answer make one way or another?

On the Project Proposal Form, you will also be asked to write about the areas you intend to cover and the resources you will need. It is easy just to write something general here (e.g. books and the Internet), but it is important, before you go too far with your Project, to make sure that you can find useful resources. In fact, you may want to spend some time researching just to check that there is helpful material that you can lay your hands on, before you finalise your proposal.

Your Project is most likely to be successful and enjoyable if you can answer yes to the following:

• Do you find the topic interesting?

• Does the topic have a link to your aims for future study or work?

• Does the topic relate to subject areas where you feel reasonably confident of your understanding?

• Does your Project title raise a question that people have strong (and different) opinions about?

• Do you have some ideas as to where you can start finding out more information about the topic?

ACTIVITY 25: WRITING A PROJECT PROPOSAL

Write a proposal for your Project. Discuss your proposal with your teacher/tutor and modify it as necessary before submitting it.

3.2 Planning the project

Research and writing

A substantial amount of work will be involved in realising your objectives and it is important to make the best use of your time. During this period, you will probably have some lessons in which you are asked to take part in particular activities or tasks which contribute to your Project, and others in which the time is made available for your own individual work.

Figure 3.1 Writing up as you go along is a good idea.

It is a good idea to write up your Project as you go along (Figure 3.1). You might want to make some changes as your work progresses, but that is better than leaving all the writing until the last minute.

A written report is a good way in which to feedback on your Project. It is worthwhile thinking about how you will format your written work – there is no 'right' way, except to say that having a good structure to your work is important. It will improve the quality of your work a great deal if you have thought about how to organise it in the most logical, easy to read, helpful way.

A simple model to use is to make sure that the written work you submit has a structure which matches the four Assessment Objectives. There should be a section about how you have planned and managed your Project, a section about your research, a section about how your Project has developed, and a section about your evaluation. Table 3.1 offers a suggested format along these lines, with some additional features, such as an abstract and introduction, which can help give your work a more professional feel.

Depending on the type of project you are working on, the amount you write will vary. The table gives recommended lengths – these are not compulsory word limits. They are based on a rough assessment of how much you would be expected to write in order to meet the Assessment Objectives. You should, however, think carefully about how well you have met the Assessment Objectives if you have written a great deal more, or a great deal less, than the amounts suggested.

If you are working on the Artefact Unit, your Project may well include a sketchbook containing visual research, photographs and development

Table 3.1 Suggested lengths for written reports

	Unit 1: Dissertation	Unit 2: Investigation/ Field Study	Unit 3: Performance	Unit 4: Artefact
Whole report	6000 words	5000 words	3000 words	1500–3000 words
Abstract/Project outline	200	100	100	50–100
Introduction	800	600	400	200–400
Research review	1850	1600	900	450–900
Discussion/Development/ Analysis	2750	2300	1350	675–1350
Conclusions/Evaluation	400	400	250	125–250
Bibliography	No word limit	No word limit	No word limit	No word limit
Appendices (e.g. Project Proposal Form, Activity Log, raw data)	No word limit	No word limit	No word limit	No word limit

sheets. The written work you produce should be linked to this. For example, you should write about the important creative decisions you have made and the reasoning which goes into these decisions. You will also need to include a written evaluation of your research and the success of your Project.

You will need to decide how much written work is needed to support any visual work you are producing. This will be different depending on the type of project, which is why a range of suggested lengths is given in Table 3.1.

Abstract/Project outline

Include:

- The project's aims
- The main ideas, arguments, and theories that you explored
- The conclusions that you reached.

Write this section last!

Introduction

Include:

- A statement of your research question or design brief: this should be an expanded and more detailed statement of your project's title
- A rationale for your choice of project objectives
- Definitions and explanations of key terms used in your Project
- An exploration of different aspects of your research question or brief.

Write a first draft of this section when you write your research question or design brief. Then come back and change or add to it as you go along.

Research review

- A survey of the source material which is relevant to your research question or design brief. While you may want to write this by simply going through the sources one at a time, a research review will be stronger if you organise the source material into a coherent narrative. A simple way of doing this is to write the review in an historical way – tracing out the main developments in chronological order.
- A critical account of the sources you have consulted. You should evaluate your source material, distinguishing where relevant between fact and opinion, and commenting on issues like influences, objectivity and reliability. All your sources should be identified and there should be full references to them in the Bibliography.

COURSE REFERENCE

Report structure and content is fully explored in Chapter 4 of this Guide.

This section is the best place to start the main work on your Project. You should also construct the Bibliography while you work on this section.

Discussion/Development/Analysis

- An account of the development of your own ideas in response to your research question or design brief. A well-written account of the development and realisation of your ideas will highlight the reasons for the point of view you have adopted, as well as addressing counter-arguments or alternative interpretations.

- If you are working on an Investigation/Field Study, this section should include discussion of your research methodology and the analysis of your data.

Start thinking about this section and making notes for it as you produce the Research Review. Start to write this section when you have more or less completed the Research Review. If you draw on any additional sources, be sure to include references to them and add them to the Bibliography.

Conclusions/Evaluation

- A statement of your conclusions and the reasoning behind them.

- An evaluation of your Project:

  - What skills have you developed during your work?

  - What have you learnt about the research process and the methodology of your Project?

  - With hindsight, what might you have done differently?

  - How might your Project be extended by further work?

Write this section when you have finished work on your Research review and Discussion/Development/Analysis. Then summarise it in a few sentences to help you write the Abstract.

Bibliography

- A list of all your information sources, presented in a clear and logical fashion and following recognised conventions, including full details of author, title, publication, publisher and date for each source.

Construct this section at the same time as you are writing the Research review and the Discussion/Development/Analysis. Then, at the end, go through it and check that it is complete and correct.

Appendices

- If you are working on an Investigation/Field Study, and you have a large amount of data, these can be included in an appendix.

- You may decide to submit your Project Proposal Form as part of an Appendix – however, if it makes more sense to place it at the front of your work, that is fine.

- You should include your Activity Log along with your written report. This is a record of your activities during the time that you were working on your Project. The focus should be on the thinking that you have done during the process: what were the key factors which affected the way your Project developed? If you have been working on the development of a performance piece, or an artefact, a lot of creative decisions will have been made. Try to represent these as clearly and succinctly as possible.

Presentation

When you have completed your Project, you will be asked to make a presentation to an audience. The presentation will contribute to the overall mark you receive for your Project. During the research period, you will have several opportunities to develop your presentation skills. Try to take full advantage of these opportunities, particularly if you are nervous about speaking to an audience. Presentation skills are something that improve with practice, and increased skill leads to increased confidence.

COURSE REFERENCE

Presentation skills will be explored in Chapter 5 of this Guide.

ACTIVITY 26: PLANNING SM

In consultation with your teacher/tutor, draw up a timetable for your Project using Table 3.2. Keep a copy in a safe and prominent place.

3.3 "Well begun is half done"

It should be self-evident that a good plan will assist you in your progress towards a successful outcome, not only with your Project, but in virtually all walks of life. Making an effective plan is a combination of experience, common sense and gathering relevant information.

How much detail?

A vague plan is not much better than no plan. Consider being given a shopping list by a friend, which says:

- Some food
- Some clothes
- Some music

Table 3.2 Project plan

Research question:

Deadline date for project report/ sketchbook/portfolio	**Date of presentation:**
Section	*Time allowed (e.g. hours/lessons/weeks)*
Project proposal and planning	
Introduction	
Research review	
Discussion/Development/Analysis	
Conclusions/Evaluation	
Abstract/Project outline	
Bibliography and final revisions	
Preparing presentation	
Week/date	*Section(s)*

Questions

1. What are the chances of coming back with what your friend actually required?

2. What would make this a better shopping list?

On the other hand, a too-prescriptive shopping list, detailing every minute requirement, but with no room for manoeuvre, may also prove unsuccessful.

The same applies to your Project – you may not end up with exactly the result you thought you would, due to extra information uncovered in your research, for instance, but your Project will be more successful in terms of breadth and depth as a result of careful planning.

Getting the right amount of detail into your plan at each stage is key to achieving a successful outcome. Good planning does not automatically result in a successful project, but bad planning inevitably results in a poor outcome.

Planning a party

Suppose you want to give a party for your brother or sister's 18th birthday. This requires a certain amount of planning if it is to run smoothly and enjoyably for all. Remember, there may be a variety of ages attending the party. Some of the key questions to ask may use the '5 W's listed below:

Who?   Why?   What?   When?   Where?

COURSE REFERENCE

You met the '5 W' questions in Chapter 1 of this Guide

ACTIVITY 27: PLANNING A PARTY   TW

In small groups, around a large sheet of paper, make a list or chart of all the possible things to be considered or done to ensure the party goes well. Take no more than 5 minutes on this exercise. Keep the sheet for future reference.

You have just 'brainstormed' the task.

Brainstorming is a good way of covering a number of points quickly, and usually involves a group of people round a table throwing in their ideas, however good or bad, or sensible or wacky, which are then jotted down for later discussion.

For the party planning activity, there will naturally be some tasks that must be done before others, e.g. buying the food before preparing and serving it. You will also know that different tasks take different amounts of time, or have to be done with suitable lead times (ahead of the final outcome).

ACTIVITY 28: DETAILING THE PLAN (TW)

Return to your record sheet from Activity 26.

Identify the logically dependant tasks. Identify any tasks that do not depend on others. Allocate suitable timings and lead times to each task, and write them on the sheet.

Keep your plan for later use.

3.4 Producing a planning chart

Charting the plan

Having made your plan, it is important to use it to check progress towards the final goal. For the party planning activity, it would probably simply involve ticking or crossing off the items as they are completed, but for your Project, it will involve setting definite milestones when the project progress is reviewed, the plan is updated, and the next target is considered in more detail. There are various techniques for doing this.

Timeline

A timeline or flow chart is a one-dimensional plan of what needs to be done, often drawn up as a vertical list of tasks, following on from each other chronologically.

Note that the timeline will be different for the different types of Extended Project (Dissertation, Investigation/Field Study, Performance or Artefact). You may already know which type you need. When you start your Project, you could add key dates and details to this chart.

A timeline is a useful guide if you are working on your own, because you can only do one thing at a time. However, in the case of the party plan exercise above, or a group project, such as a theatrical performance, several of you may be working on different tasks simultaneously. This would need planning on a two-dimensional chart. In that case, it may be more useful to use a PERT chart or Gantt chart to plan and monitor progress.

PERT chart

Figure 3.2 shows a PERT (Program Evaluation and Review Technique) chart. Along each task, shown by coloured arrows, are the times taken in months. The key points are simply numbered from 10 to 50 (to allow for extra detail), but could be called stage 1, stage 2, etc.

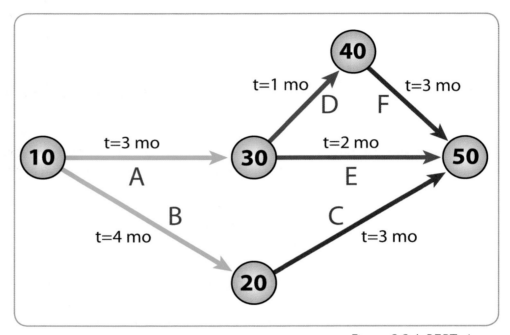

Figure 3.2 A PERT chart

Originally developed to manage complex military projects, the PERT chart shows how the various stages relate, and, in particular, which are the critical tasks. In Figure 3.2, task E is the least critical in terms of time taken – it could take up to four months without upsetting the whole programme.

However, the detail of each stage and the 'time now' is less obviously shown.

Gantt chart

Developed in the 1930s to assist project planning, the Gantt chart is a useful and common way of planning and monitoring the progress of a project.

The chart usually shows a timescale across the top and a list of jobs down the side, as shown in Figure 3.3.

Notice how the dependence of one job on another is shown by vertical arrows, progress is shown by coloured-in sections, and the 'today' line is shown dotted.

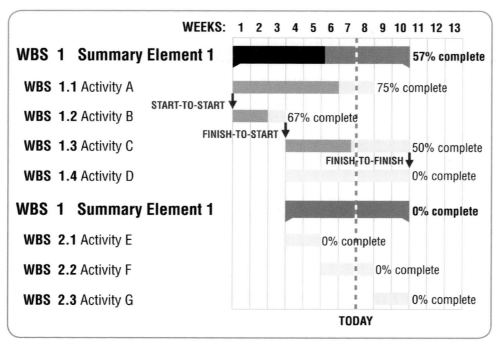

Figure 3.3 A Gantt chart.

You will find examples of this layout on the Internet, and you can use Excel to generate your own chart.

Computer or paper?

The advantage of using a computer to create a Gantt chart is that extra tasks can easily be added, and times modified as required. The grid can be coloured in to represent the tasks, and the colours can be changed as the task progresses, making it very clear at a glance how the project is progressing.

However, the computer should only be used where it enhances the planning process and helps to communicate the plan. All original creative work, brainstorming, etc., should be done with pencil and paper to facilitate the flow of ideas straight onto the page. Some projects, particularly those involving artistic or technical design, are best done freely on paper initially, and it may be a good idea to always carry a notebook with you so you can jot ideas down as they occur to you.

If you find yourself taking hours trying to construct a chart or drawing on the computer, ask yourself if there is an easier way to communicate your ideas. You can always photograph or scan a hand-drawn design into your computer document.

Remember, the computer is a tool to help you and it should not hinder your progress.

ACTIVITY 29: PRODUCING A GANTT CHART

Using a spreadsheet programme such as Excel, or a sheet of lined or squared paper, produce your own Gantt chart to show the steps involved in planning your party.

Make a scale of days or dates across the top, and a detailed list of the jobs down the left-hand side. Allocate timings to each task by colouring the cells.

Decide how your chart could be used to show the ongoing progress.

3.5 Planning and managing project work

When the time comes to start your Project, you will need to think about how you are going to plan your time allocation, using some of the ideas discussed above.

To plan a large project effectively, it is necessary to break it down into manageable smaller tasks – a bite-sized approach. This basic process has several advantages. It:

• helps you think through the whole project in outline

• makes the project more manageable and less daunting

• focuses your attention on each task in a logical sequence.

All the Extended Projects have the same overall objectives, which are detailed in the Specification and summarised below. You should be able to:

• identify, plan and manage the project

• use resources to research and select data and information

• develop and realise, to achieve the planned outcomes

• review and evaluate the outcomes in a presentation.

In your Project Proposal Form, you will have outlined the objectives and activities you expect to undertake, and the resources that you will need. Your teacher/tutor will be able to give you a copy of the Assessment Objectives and weightings for the type of Extended Project you are doing, and the key dates for the final project completion and presentation.

ACTIVITY 30: PLANNING YOUR PROJECT

Decide what the main stages of your Project are. Ask your teacher/tutor for the key dates and the milestone assessment points. Then construct your own Gantt chart for the project.

Naturally, you cannot identify all the problems that may crop up, so building in some slack to allow for setbacks is recommended at this stage.

You may want to print off your Gantt chart and have it at the front of your project file or above your desk, or you could keep it on the computer so that changes can be made and progress recorded.

Managing your Project

It is important to refer to your chart regularly, updating where necessary, and noting when you appear to be falling behind schedule.

Your teacher/tutor should monitor your progress with you and help identify, in good time, any missed deadlines or remedial action to be taken.

The Project Activity Record

You must also maintain a Project Activity Record, which documents your progress, the activities you undertake and the decisions you make. This can be in the form of a diary or log, and a suggested outline is shown (Table 3.3).

You should take a few minutes at the start of the week planning what to do, and a few minutes at the end outlining what you actually did. This record should be available for review by your teacher at appropriate times.

Table 3.3 Project Activity Record

Week	What I plan to do	What I actually did
1		
2		
3		

The Project Activity Record has two purposes: to help you keep on schedule and to give you a framework as you write up your Project.

4 Execution

4.1 Getting started

The Introduction

Whatever type of project you are carrying out, you will need to provide a report of your work. You can use the structure of the report to help you organise and manage your project work. You will be able to focus on different aspects of your Project and write some of the report as you go along, which is much better than leaving the writing as a major task to be done right at the end.

If your Project is a dissertation or an investigation, the report will be the main outcome. For other Extended Projects, the report will accompany an artefact or a performance, and will provide a record and critical evaluation of what you did. In all cases, your report should be structured under headings (see Table 3.1 in Lesson 3.2). This structure will help other people to read and understand the report, as well as helping you to organise your work.

The Introduction is the first main section of your report. Its purpose is to set the scene for your readers and draw them in to the report. Drafting the Introduction at an early stage can also help focus your own mind on your topic; then, as you gather information and refine your ideas, you can come back and revise your draft.

In completing your Project Proposal Form, you will have already done some work towards your Project. Turning your Project Proposal Form into the first draft of your Introduction is a good way to get started on your report.

Your Introduction should have three main subsections.

Project topic or research question

As you begin work on your Project, write a few sentences saying what you intend to do. During your Project, you might find that your work develops in ways that you did not anticipate. For your final report, you will need to rewrite your Introduction to describe the work you actually did. Any major changes of direction should be noted in the Conclusion/Evaluation at the end of your report, where you reflect on the way your work developed during the project.

Rationale and background

This is probably the longest subsection of your Introduction. To start, you should explain why you chose your project topic/research question. (Perhaps a personal experience has drawn your attention to a particular issue. Maybe your Project relates to an intended future career, or an area where you particularly want to develop your skills. Or maybe you read something, or saw a TV programme, that started you thinking about a particular topic.)

You should also outline the background to your Project and note any relevant issues, such as ethical questions or other areas of controversy (you might do this as you are explaining why you chose your particular topic/research question). This is an opportunity to demonstrate your knowledge of some of the terminology that you have learnt earlier in the course and refer to relevant ethical frameworks.

Definitions of key terms

Here you should note and define any key terms that you use in your report. Some of these might be unfamiliar technical terms that you come across during your research, but others will be 'everyday' terms (such as 'rights' or 'life') whose meaning needs to be made clear in the context of your Project. Use dictionaries to help you, and try also to clarify the meanings by giving examples and '**criteria** for use'.

> **ACTIVITY 31: DRAFTING THE INTRODUCTION**
>
> Consider your project topic/research question and write a draft Introduction, using the guidelines above and those given in Table 3.1. Keep this draft in a safe place. As you prepare your final report, return to your draft and modify it accordingly.

4.2 Research review

The Research review

It is best to start the main work on your Project by gathering some information and working on the Research review section of your report. The work you do here will also contribute to the Discussion/Evaluation/Analysis section.

The Research review is a summary of the background to your Project and an account of other work that has already been published that relates to your topic. It is essentially an account of who did what, and what they have written (or said) about the topic. As far as possible, put the information in your own words rather than copying straight from the source.

A good Research review should tell a coherent 'story'. You can only really do this, however, after your have consulted several sources and found out what

> **COURSE REFERENCE**
>
> You met ethical frameworks in Activities 10, 11, 12 and 13 in Chapter 2 of this Guide.

> **COURSE REFERENCE**
>
> Lesson 2.7 in Chapter 2 of this Guide is about the careful use of language and techniques for defining terms.

Figure 4.1 Visiting the Salford University library.

they contain. To start with, it is a good idea to keep a separate page of notes (either paper or electronic) for each source you consult. Then, when you have consulted several sources (Figure 4.1), you can start to sort your notes into a logical order and put them together to make your Research review.

Use Table 4.1 to help you plan your work for this part of your Project.

Table 4.1 Planning the Research review

Project topic or research question	
What will you research? Consider the 'story', context, key individuals and dates, influences on the principal characters. Also consider source evaluation (reliability, primary or secondary, fact, speculation or opinion)	
What sources will you use? Consider libraries, museums, websites, people worth talking to	
What will you do? Collecting materials, note-taking, compiling the Bibliography, assembling the Research review, editing, adding evaluation of sources, further research	
Deadline (date)	

Week (date)	Actions

Getting started

Here are some things to think about before you start.

• Where will you begin to look for information?

• Are there some useful books in your school/college library?

• Do you know of any relevant websites?

• Are there people or organisations that might be able to give you information? How do you plan to contact or visit them?

• Might you be able to find relevant items in newspapers or magazines or from TV programmes?

For each information source that you use, keep a careful record of the following. You will need this information for your Bibliography and in case you want to revisit the same source later.

• Full details of the source.

• For books and articles: the author(s), title, publisher and date.

• For websites: the full URL, the name(s) of the person or organisation that produced the site (if available) and the date when you consulted the site.

• For any relevant quotes within the source: full details of their origin.

• A summary of the relevant information that it contains – look for the '5 W' questions: *who, what, where, why, when* (and *how*).

COURSE REFERENCE

You met the '5 W' questions in Chapter 1 of this Guide.

• A summary of any relevant arguments used or quoted by the authors:

  - What assumptions are being made?

  - Is the argument valid?

  - Are there any flaws?

  - What is the ideological or philosophical position adopted?

  - What ethical framework is being used?

COURSE REFERENCE

You met ethical frameworks in Activities 10, 11, 12 and 13.

• A brief review of the nature of the source:

  - Is it a primary or secondary source?

  - Does it contain reliable fact, subjective opinion or speculation?

  - Could the author(s) have a vested interest, and might they be biased?

COURSE REFERENCE

Lessons 1.2 and 1.4 describe various types of source material.

ACTIVITY 32: STARTING THE RESEARCH REVIEW

Choose three information sources that you have consulted and write an account of how they contribute to your Project.

Later, as you consult more sources and your Project develops, you can modify and add to this account and hence produce your Research review.

4.3 Good communication

Written communication

Some of the marks for your Project will be given for the quality of your written communication. When consulting source materials for your Project, you probably found some that were clear and easy to read, and others that were more difficult. Of course, the 'difficulty' of a piece of text depends partly on its content, but the way it is written and presented can also make a huge difference to whether it is easy to read and understand.

COURSE REFERENCE

The style in which a report is written can affect the way readers respond to it. See, for example, Activity 3.

Your experience of reading other people's work should help you with your own writing. You should aim to make your report as clear and readable as possible. You want your readers to know what you have done and what you have found out. Also, your readers should be able to follow your arguments and to understand your point of view.

ACTIVITY 33: WRITTEN COMMUNICATION

Figure 4.2 lists various features that might make a project report easier, or more difficult, to read. Work in a small group to sort these features into three categories: those that, in your experience, make a long piece of text easier to read and understand, those that make it more difficult or off-putting, and those that make no difference. Then write a checklist of points to look out for in your own report.

short, clear sentences

no clear structure (the writer keeps losing track of where he or she is going – and so do you)

lots of unexplained unfamiliar words to keep you guessing

text organised under main headings and subheadings

summaries of important points (the writer is sure about what he/she wants to tell you)

long sentences with little or no punctuation (the writer is really making you work hard)

lots of rambling repetition (is the writer not worried about boring or confusing you?)

contradictions and inconsistencies (how do you know what the writer really means?)

short, clear paragraphs

a logical development with a clear beginning, middle and end

'signposting' to alert you to what's coming next (e.g 'There are three key ideas here: first...')

colourful illustrations

numbered pages

clear explanations of unfamiliar words and ideas

a quirky style with lots of slang words to show how cool the writer is (cool or annoying?)

very small print and narrow margins

a pompous style with lots of long words and long sentences to show how clever the writer is (or thinks he/she is)

Figure 4.2 Factors affecting the readability of a report.

COURSE REFERENCE

In Thinking skills Lesson 2.7 you used various techniques to define and clarify key terms.

ACTIVITY 34: WELL WRITTEN?

As you write your report, bear in mind your checklist from Activity 32 and try to write as clearly as possible. When you have written a section, put it aside for a day and then reread it. Something that you thought was very clear when you first wrote it might not read quite so well when you come to it with fresh eyes.

If possible, exchange drafts with someone else in your class. Try to give one another polite but honest feedback on readability, then act upon it.

4.4 All my own work

Whose work is it anyway?

Using someone else's work and pretending it is your own is called **plagiarism**. It is a form of cheating. For example, a researcher who 'borrowed' someone else's results and published them under their own name would be committing plagiarism.

ACTIVITY 35: WHOSE WORK IS IT ANYWAY?

In a small group, discuss situations in which plagiarism might occur.

Figure 4.3 Raj Persaud

Any writer or researcher who is found to have plagiarised someone else's work is likely to have their career and reputation permanently damaged or destroyed. Author Dan Brown was accused of plagiarising someone else's work to write his best-selling novel *The Da Vinci Code*, and in spring of 2006 he fought – and won – a long and expensive court case to clear his name and reputation. In June 2008, the General Medical Council (GMC) found media psychiatrist Dr Raj Persaud (Figure 4.3) guilty of plagiarising the work of other academics in some of his books and articles. Raj Persaud admitted he had not taken enough care when referring to other people's work. He had asked for their permission and included their names in the acknowledgments, but had not clearly indicated which passages were not his own original work. The GMC suspended him for three months, which meant he was not allowed to work as a psychiatrist during that period.

ACTIVITY 36: WHAT'S WRONG WITH PLAGIARISM?

Plagiarism is regarded as a serious wrongdoing. Discuss reasons for this and consider how you might use various ethical frameworks to make the case against (or in favour of) plagiarism.

COURSE REFERENCE

You met ethical frameworks in Chapters 2.2 and 2.3 of this Guide. See Activities 10, 11, 12 and 13.

Avoiding plagiarism

By now, it will probably be obvious where this is leading: your own Project. Plagiarism is a potential issue with any written coursework, and it is important that you understand what is, and is not, acceptable. As well as reading this Guide, you should also read the relevant parts of the Extended Project Specification.

The Internet is a huge resource and contains not only 'raw material' for research but websites from which it is possible to obtain entire essays and projects. *It is most important that you resist the temptation to paste such material into your own project.* In addition to the ethical aspect, such material is likely to be detected by your teacher/tutor, with serious consequences – your Project could be disqualified. And when you come to give your presentation, you will find it difficult to answer questions about work you have copied from elsewhere while pretending to have done it yourself.

Deliberate plagiarism as described above is easy to avoid: just don't do it. But, in practice, plagiarism is more likely to be accidental. In your Project, you are expected to use a range of resources to gather information and to help you discuss your topic or research question. 'Research' does not mean 'developing absolutely everything from scratch'. Indeed, the very nature of the project means that you will need to draw on a large body of existing literature and synthesise your own work from the work of others together with your own ideas.

There is absolutely nothing wrong with quoting exactly what somebody else has said or written – but the key term here is 'quoting'. Any material quoted from elsewhere should be clearly indicated either by quotation marks or by consistently using a different font, and full details of the source should be given either in the main text (e.g. using footnotes) or in the Bibliography. (For example, material quoted in this Guide is always distinguished from the rest of the text and is always followed immediately by details of the source.) Only if quoted material is 'hidden' and passed off as your own original work does quoting become plagiarism.

4.5 Bibliography and footnotes

This lesson shows you two techniques that are widely used by authors of academic books and articles. You should aim to use both while writing your report.

Bibliography

A **bibliography** is a list of all the sources referred to in a project, essay or research paper. It is usually placed at the end under the heading 'Bibliography' or 'References'. Its purpose is to make clear to readers exactly how other people's work has been used, and to enable readers to consult the same sources themselves if they wish to.

When you draw on or refer to work from another source (Figure 4.4), this must be made clear in the main text (otherwise you are probably committing plagiarism) and you must give clear details to enable readers to find the same source.

Bibliography

K. Ansell-Pearson & D. Large, *The Nietzsche Reader*. Blackwell, Oxford (2005).

D. Cadbury, *The Dinosaur Hunters*. Fourth Estate, London (2001).

W. Ellwood & J. McMurty, *The No-nonsense Guide to Globalisation*. New Internationalist Publications (2001).

E. Evans, *The Birth of Modern Britain 1780–1914*. Longman, London (1997).

L. Freedman, *Atlas of Global Strategy*. Macmillan, London (1985).

A. Hunt & R. Millar, *AS Science for Public Understanding*. Heinemann, Oxford (2000).

E. Nisbet, *Getting heated over glaciation*. Nature 422, 812–813 (2003).

R. Rees, *Poverty and Public Health 1815–1948*. Heinemann, Oxford (2001).

M. B. Steger, *Globalization: A Very Short Introduction*. Oxford University Press, Oxford (2003)

Figure 4.4 All sources must be referenced in a Bibliography.

There are two main conventions for organising references: alphabetical and numerical. An advantage of the alphabetical system is that readers can immediately get some information about the source you have used without having to turn to another page. An advantage of the numerical system is that it is a bit more compact, particularly when referring to websites.

For your Project, choose whichever convention you prefer and stick to it consistently.

Alphabetical

In the main text, where you quote or refer to a printed source, give the surname(s) of the author(s) in brackets followed by the year of publication, e.g. (Close, 1990) or (Pears and Shields, 2004). If there are three or more authors, it is usual just to list the first one then 'et al.' (meaning 'and others'), e.g. (Cobley et al., 2006). If you are referring to a website, the brackets should contain the author, if known, and the URL of the home page, e.g. (Atyiah, www.bmj.com).

In your Bibliography, each reference should be given as shown below.

For books:

> Surname, Initials (Year) *Name of book in italic*, Publisher, Place of publication, Chapter number, Page number(s)

Publication details are usually printed on the reverse of the title page at the front of the book.

For journals (or magazines):

> Surname, Initials (Year) Title of article, *Name of journal in italic*, **Volume number (issue number if applicable) in bold**, Page number(s)

Details of volume and issue number are usually given on the contents page and/or in the header or footer running along each page.

For websites:

> Author or editor (Year) *Title* [online]. Publisher, Place of publication. Available from: URL [Date of access]

Ideally, your reference should contain all these details, but, in practice, many websites do not include such full information, so include as much as you can find. Sometimes the 'author' is an organisation rather than a named person.

In your Bibliography, sources should be listed in alphabetical order of surname of first author, regardless of the order in which they relate to your main text.

For example:

> Atiyah, M. (1999) *Science for evil: the scientist's dilemma* [online]. British Medical Journal, London. Available from: www.bmj. bmjjournals.com/cgi/content/full/319/7207/448 [accessed 27 October 2008]

> Holmes, B. (2004) Squeeze gently to clone monkeys, *New Scientist*, **184 (2477)**, p. 8.

> Pears, R and Shields, G. (2005) *Cite them right: The essential guide to referencing and plagiarism*. Pear Tree Books.

> Royal Society (2004) *The use of non-human animals in research: a guide for scientists* [online]. Royal Society, London. Available from: www.royalsoc.ac.uk/displaypagedoc.asp?id=10298 [accessed 27 October 2008]

Numerical

In the main text, refer to sources by numbers in either square brackets [1] or superscripts[1] – use either one or the other system, not a mixture. The first source you refer to is [1], the second [2], and so on. If you need to refer to the same source later, use the same number as before.

The references are then listed in numerical order in your Bibliography. The conventions for listing names of authors and publications are similar to the alphabetical system. The differences are that the initials come before the surnames and the publication years are put in a different place.

For example:

1. B. Holmes, Squeeze gently to clone monkeys, *New Scientist*, 2004, **184 (2477)**, p. 8.

2. M. Atiyah, *Science for evil: the scientist's dilemma* [online], 1999. British Medical Journal, London. Available from: www.bmj. bmjjournals.com/cgi/content/full/319/7207/448 [accessed 27 October 2008]

3. R. Pears and G. Shields, *Cite them right: The essential guide to referencing and plagiarism*, 2005, Pear Tree Books.

4. Royal Society, *The use of non-human animals in research: a guide for scientists* [online], 2004. Royal Society, London. Available from: www.royalsoc.ac.uk/displaypagedoc.asp?id=10298 [accessed 27 October 2008]

ACTIVITY 37: REFERENCES

Look at some examples of publications and notice how they refer to other sources.

Use one of the conventions described above to produce references for a selection of printed and web-based materials. Ideally, use sources that you are consulting for your Project.

Footnotes

The point of a footnote, in an academic document, is to provide supplementary information without interrupting the main flow of the text. Specifically, footnotes may be used to provide such information as:

- details of a reference – either textual or web-based. This is particularly helpful if the reference is lengthy, as it will be if it is a full URL

- comments on a source which has been used in the text

- comments on the main argument.

Suppose, for example, that you were making an argument about the rights of animals. You may well have chosen a particular definition for the term 'rights', and, in a footnote, you might explain that this was your own choice and that other people have different definitions. The footnote could also contain a reference so that the reader can follow up these other definitions, if they so wish.

When writing your Research review, footnotes are a sensible place for the evaluation of your sources. If you incorporate all the information about whether your source is primary or secondary; whether it contains facts, speculation or opinion; and whether it is objective or biased in the flow of the text, it will distract the reader from the main point. On the other hand, leaving it to the end makes it seem disconnected from your 'story'. This is an ideal opportunity to show that you can make good use of footnotes.

Footnotes are usually indicated by superscript letters or numbers which refer the reader to additional information at the foot of the page. Most word-processing packages allow you to insert footnotes very easily[a]. If you are using the numerical convention for your Bibliography, make sure you don't have two confusing numbering systems: use letters for your footnotes and/or use numbers in square brackets for your references.

---

[a] If you are using Word on a PC, you will find footnotes by selecting 'Insert' on the main toolbar, then selecting 'Reference' followed by 'Footnote'.

ACTIVITY 38: FOOTNOTES

Select one page of your Research review, or mini-review if you have not yet begun writing the main thing. Insert some footnotes to do some of the tasks listed above.

4.6 What are you doing? What do you think?

After the Research review comes the main 'meat' of your Project: the Development, Discussion or Analysis section of your report.

If you are working on an investigation or field study, this section might be subdivided under headings such as Method and Results and will include some or all of the following:

- a description and/or diagrams of apparatus that you use, including anything that you make or modify yourself

- a description and/or map of your fieldwork location(s)

- details of your method

- graphs or charts presenting your data (not all your raw data – that goes into an Appendix)

- an account of how you analyse your data

- your final results.

If you are producing an artefact, this section might be subdivided under headings such as Development and Analysis, and will include:

- details of any materials that you use

- an account of the techniques that you try out and select.

If you are developing a performance, this section might be subdivided under headings such as Development and Analysis, and will include:

- a description of how the performance is developed, and your own role in it

- an account of how your group's approach changes as you work through the project

- details of any source materials

- information about the venue

- information about the audience

- details of any technical resources.

If you are working on a dissertation, this section will probably be headed Discussion, and will include:

• a statement of your own point of view on your research question

• arguments and counter-arguments relating to your point of view.

For *all* Extended Projects, this section needs to include an account of your own ideas and your own **point of view** in response to your research question or design brief.

What's the point of a point of view?

If you look back to the Project Proposal Form that you filled in before beginning your Project, you will remember that you specified a particular research question or design brief. Ideally, you chose this because you found it interesting and worth studying. It is likely that you have a point of view on your topic – for example, you think one particular answer to the question is true, or you have views about how best to tackle a performance. Perhaps you are cautious and would prefer just to say that one approach or answer is better than another. However you express it, your Project will be much stronger if you can identify clearly what you really think about your topic. You need to have a clearly defined point of view.

When taking part in an argument (Figure 4.5), some people can only see things from their own point of view. They cannot understand the opposite side of the debate at all. At the other extreme, some people shrug their shoulders and decide that we can never know what to believe, since there are always good arguments on both sides of the debate.

Figure 4.5 Discussing points of view

COURSE REFERENCE

Much of Chapter 2 of this book is devoted to developing thinking skills and setting out arguments relating to a point of view.

The best approach lies between these extremes. In the Discussion or Analysis section of your report, you should definitely consider arguments on both sides of any debate. Doing this is part of recognising that people who think deeply about the issues still come to different conclusions. However, it is also important that you form a view of your own and try to defend it. It might seem as though you are being fairer by just stating both sides of the argument. In reality, though, you will learn more and understand the issues better if you try to argue for your own point of view. It is when you do this that you will discover where the real strengths and weaknesses in your ideas lie.

ACTIVITY 39: IDENTIFYING A POINT OF VIEW

Reread your Project Proposal Form and briefly explain to others in your class what your topic is, what your research question is, and what your own ideas are.

Clarifying your point of view

People hold all sorts of opinions on ethical and other questions, but their ideas are often quite vague. A central skill which you will be expected to demonstrate in the Analysis or Discussion section of your Project is that of expressing your point of view clearly. This is a skill which you began to develop when you looked at how to define key words.

Example 1

Suppose you are writing a dissertation about embryonic stem cell research. You will need to define each of these words:

- Embryonic: what is an embryo? Is it the same as a foetus? Is an embryo a human being? Is an embryo an individual? Is an embryo a person?

- Stem cell: what are stem cells? How are they different from other cells? Can there be different types of stem cell?

- Research: what types of activity do scientists do with embryonic stem cells? Is research different from medical treatment? Could some research also involve treatment?

As well as thinking about the definitions of key words, you can clarify your point of view by considering the viewpoint of those whom you disagree with. This is one reason why it is important to have a viewpoint of your own – you can sharpen your ideas by contrasting them with opposing viewpoints.

Example 2

Suppose your point of view is that embryonic stem cell research is a good idea. This is a point of view which you could defend in your Project. But, before you started arguing for it, you would need to clarify exactly what it is that you believe.

• Do you think every type of embryonic stem cell research is a good idea?

• Do you think that some types are acceptable and others not?

• What do the opponents of such research believe?

• Do you disagree with them completely or are there some cases where you agree?

Asking questions such as these can help to clarify your point of view.

It is also helpful to think about what general ethical and/or philosophical frameworks you accept. In the Thinking skills chapter of this Guide, you looked at common ethical frameworks, including utilitarianism, divine commands, rights and virtues. When you are thinking about your point of view on an ethical question, you should consider which of these frameworks you accept. You can then classify your position – you will know where you stand in the debate.

> **COURSE REFERENCE**
>
> For a summary of commonly used ethical frameworks, see Chapter 2 of this Guide.

Example 3

Suppose you decide to defend the point of view that embryonic stem cell research, up to a certain time limit and for certain purposes, is acceptable. Why do you think this? Is it because of utilitarian reasons (this research will bring more benefit than any harm it involves)? Or is it because you have thought about the rights involved and think that embryos up to a certain time limit do not have rights? Perhaps you prefer to adopt the divine command theory – in which case, your point of view will be a religious one.

When you have thought about such questions as these, you will be able to describe and explain your viewpoint more clearly (e.g. "I adopt a utilitarian viewpoint", "My viewpoint is religious", "My viewpoint is based on rights").

ACTIVITY 40: WHAT DO THEY THINK?

Using a copy of the questionnaire in Table 4.2, work with another learner and interview one another about your Projects and your points of view (Figure 4.6). When you are the interviewer, write your partner's answers in the spaces provided in the questionnaire. Then make some suggestions about what they could do to make their point of view clearer still. Bear in mind that this is a constructive exercise – you are not aiming to criticise someone else's ideas just for the sake of being critical.

Figure 4.6
Interviewing a peer

ACTIVITY 41: WHAT DO YOU THINK?　E

Write a summary of the answers you have given to the interview questions and a short response to the comments made by your interviewer about how your point of view could be made clearer.

Table 4.2 Thinking clearly about points of view

Name of interviewer:	Name of interviewee:

1. What is the interviewee's research question?

2. What is the interviewee's point of view about their research question?

3. What are the key words they have used in describing their point of view?

4. How do they define each of these key words?

5. What viewpoints does the interviewee disagree with?

6. What ethical frameworks does the interviewee use when defending their point of view?

7. In what ways could the interviewee make their point of view clearer or more precise?

4.7 Discussing discussions

The Analysis or Discussion

The Analysis or Discussion section of your report is where you describe your own point of view and explain why you believe it. This means defining, as clearly as possible, what it is you believe, then trying to find arguments in favour of your viewpoint, as well as answers to arguments against (Figure 4.7).

Figure 4.7 Discussing discussions

What is the difference between the Discussion/Analysis section and the Research review? The Research review looks mainly at the background material for your Project, considering who did what and what they have written (or said) about the topic. It also involves assessing the reliability of the source materials which you are using. In the Discussion section, you will also want to make use of source material but for a different purpose. The source material will mainly refer to arguments and issues related to your project topic. Your aim will be to analyse these arguments critically and to build up a strong case for your own point of view. This will involve presenting arguments in favour of your point of view, as well as considering and trying to answer objections.

Use Table 4.3 to help you plan your work for this part of your Project.

> **COURSE REFERENCE**
>
> The Thinking skills part of the course is particularly relevant to the Discussion section of your report.

Table 4.3 Discussion planner

Research question	
Central ideas and ethical theories that people use to answer your question	
Statement of your point of view	
Supporting lines of argument for your point of view	
Objections to your point of view	
Response to objections	
General comments about the limitations of your case	

ACTIVITY 42: ANALYSING THE NEWS

Working in a small group or with a partner, look through a recent edition of a newspaper.

Find an article in which the author is arguing for their particular point of view. Make notes using the headings from Table 4.3 to help you analyse the author's arguments. (Your headings should refer to the author's point of view, arguments, and so on – rather than your own.)

Write a letter to the newspaper replying to the author of the argument you have read. Before doing this, it may be helpful to look at how letters to the paper are written. They tend to be brief (no more than 400 words). They contain criticism of the author's arguments and usually a defence of the letter writer's point of view. You should aim to write in a style appropriate to the newspaper you have read.

4.8 Conclusion or Evaluation

Reaching a conclusion

The purpose of the Conclusion or Evaluation of your report is to look back and to look forwards. Looking back means summarising what you have investigated, developed or argued for: what you have found out through your laboratory or fieldwork; how your skills have developed; what your point of view is and how you have tried to argue your case. It also means looking back to see how your ideas and understanding have changed. It may be that your point of view has altered, either because you have changed your mind or because you have learned to define your position more clearly. Perhaps you have gained new insight into a creative process, or changed the way you understand a phenomenon that you investigated.

Look back at your original Project Proposal Form and to the first draft of your Introduction (Lesson 4.1) and reflect on the ways your Project developed. Even if you have not changed your ideas or your point of view, you will almost certainly have learned more about the investigation, and/or creative processes, and/or arguments for and against your position. The Conclusion/Evaluation provides you with an opportunity to step back and put all of this experience into context. You will have learnt a great deal, not just about your particular topic, but about the nature of research, creativity and debate.

The emphasis of the Evaluation or Conclusion will depend to some extent on the nature of your Project. For an investigation or field study, you will focus on the research process and how your knowledge and understanding have changed. Part of your evaluation will involve reviewing your apparatus and/or methodology and considering how these might be modified. For a dissertation, the emphasis will be on the process of research and argument, and how your point of view has developed. For a performance or an artefact, you will consider what you have learnt about creative processes (probably including group work in the case of performance), and how your ideas and skills have developed. Your evaluation will include some reflection on what you might have done differently with hindsight.

ACTIVITY 43: THE STORY OF YOUR PROJECT

Working with another learner, take it in turns to interview one another in order to help tell the story of your Project (Figure 4.8). Don't worry about making notes. The aim of the exercise is to give one another a chance to think about how the process has gone – how your ideas have changed and what you have learnt about research and creativity. It is not easy to do this kind of thinking (the technical name is 'metacognition' – thinking about thinking). You will need to be a patient and helpful interviewer.

The key questions to address (along with others if you find them helpful) are:

- How have your ideas and/or skills developed during the course of the project?

- Can you summarise your initial point of view and the case you have made for it?

- What have you learnt about the process of carrying out your Project?

- If you could continue your Project, what further work would you do?

Figure 4.8 Interviewing can help you clarify your Conclusion.

ACTIVITY 44: TELLING YOUR STORY

Your experience in Activity 42 will have helped you reflect on the work you have done for your Project. A good Evaluation is one in which this story is also well presented. Working with a different partner, tell the story of your Project. You should cover all the points that have come up in the course of your interview:

- how your ideas have developed in the course of the project

- a summary of your point of view

- what you have learnt about the creative process

- what you have learnt about doing research

- what further work you could do.

ACTIVITY 45: WRITING YOUR STORY

Write the story of your Project, making sure that you answer all the key questions asked in Activity 42. What you write will form the basis of the Conclusion or Evaluation of your Project.

4.9 Outline

Abstract questions

In carrying out your Research review, you may have come across articles that begin with a short outline, often called an **abstract**, summarising their key points. Academic journal articles generally include an abstract. In other types of publication, it might be called an outline or summary. Whatever you call it, you should provide one for your report as it will help give your work a more professional feel.

ACTIVITY 46: ABSTRACT QUESTIONS

In a small group, spend a few minutes discussing the following questions.

- What do you think is the purpose of an abstract?

- Who is it written for?

- What are some key features of a good abstract?

For your Project, aim to write a short outline or abstract summarising your work. Although it is placed at the start of your report, you should write it last! After you have written the report, write an abstract that summarises the main points of your Project, then read carefully through your work and make sure that the abstract really does reflect what the report says.

COURSE REFERENCE

See Table 3.1 for suggested length.

ACTIVITY 47: WRITING AN ABSTRACT

Read carefully through an article or a book chapter and write an abstract in no more than 250 words summing up its main points.

Compare your abstract with one written by someone else for the same article or chapter. Discuss any similarities and differences between what each has written and try to come to an agreement about what should, or should not, be included in the abstract. Then revise your own abstract as you feel necessary.

4.10 The final report

The final report

When you have written all the sections of your report, you will want to edit it to make sure that it reads well, that you have clearly described what you did and what you achieved or discovered, that your point of view is clear and that the main lines of your argument can be clearly followed. There are two aspects to this: content and communication. In other words, what you have written and the way you have written it. Your Project will be assessed on both these aspects. Activities 32 and 33 (Lesson 4.3) referred to communication, and you might like to revisit them as you prepare your final draft. Here you are concerned with the content of your report and the way it is organised.

ACTIVITY 48: EDITING

Use the checklists below to make sure your report contains everything that it needs to, and that things are in the correct sections.

Abstract/Outline

- Have you stated the main result of your investigation or field study, or the point of view you defend in your dissertation?

- Have you stated the key features of your artefact or performance?

- Have you outlined the aims, methods, arguments and conclusions of your Project?

- Is your abstract in a logical order?

- Have you related your Project to the main theories relevant to your topic?

Introduction

- Do you have a well-defined design brief or research question?

- Have you stated your rationale for your choice of question or topic?

- Have you described the ethical and other controversial aspects of your question?

- Have you given an analysis of the key terms used in your Project?

- Is your Introduction well structured?

- Does your Introduction lead into your Project?

- Have you explained how your Project fits into discussion of your topic?

Research review

- Have you chosen material which provides an original context for your Project?

- Have you given a detailed outline of the 'story'?

- Do you include key dates and people involved in the story?

- Do you discuss the influences on any principal characters?

- Have you evaluated the reliability of your sources?

- Have you considered which sources are primary and which are secondary?

- Have you distinguished between fact, speculation and opinion?

Development/ Discussion/Analysis

- Have you clearly described what you did?

- Have you given details of any apparatus, raw materials or technical resources that you used?

- Have you described the creative development of your artefact or performance and the processes that you went through?

- For a group performance, have you clearly described your own role?

- For an investigation or field study, have you described your data analysis and presented your results?

- Is your point of view on key questions relating to your Project defined using terms drawn from central theories (such as ethical frameworks, or theories relating to performance practice)?

- Have you given supporting arguments for your point of view?

- Have you considered and responded to objections to your point of view?

- Do the different parts of the discussion link together to form an integrated case?

- Is your Development/Discussion/Analysis logically presented and have you been careful to use language precisely throughout?

Conclusions/Evaluation

- For an investigation or field study, have you stated the main thing that you discovered?

- Have you given a clear summary of your point of view?

- Have you reflected on how your skills and ideas have developed during the course of the project?

- Have you explained what you have learnt about the creative process and/or research?

- Have you included ideas about possible extensions to your Project?

References and Bibliography

- Have you included references to all your sources?

- Have you used a consistent system of references throughout the report?

- Do you use footnotes to provide additional information?

- Is your Bibliography properly constructed (listing author, title, publisher, publication date, edition number and page numbers)?

Appendices

- Have you included your original Project Proposal Form?

- Have you included your Activity Log? Is it complete and up to date?

- For an investigation or field study, have you included all your raw data?

- For a performance, have you included all items such as rehearsal schedules, notes on rehearsals, records of meetings?

- For an artefact, have you included evidence of the development process, such as sketches or notebooks?

General

- Is your report within the suggested word limit (Table 3.1)?

- Have you checked the spelling?

5 Presentation

5.1 Show and tell

Planning a presentation

You will be asked to give a presentation on your Project and answer questions on your work from your teacher/tutor (and maybe from another expert). The presentation can take various forms, including:

• an oral presentation (Figure 5.1) of about 10 minutes to a live audience

• an oral presentation that you video for your teacher/tutor to watch later

• a display where you are on hand to answer questions about your work.

It is a good idea to start thinking about your presentation while you are working on the Development or Discussion section of your report, though the main work will probably take place after you have finished your written report.

Figure 5.1 Oral presentation

Regardless of the format, your presentation will be assessed according to these questions.

• Is it clearly and logically structured?

• If oral, is it audible throughout?

• Are your visual aids or displayed items relevant and helpful?

• Are they well designed, clear, and not cluttered with too much information?

• Do you respond calmly and confidently to questions?

• Do your answers show insight and good subject knowledge?

The activities in this lesson and the next two will help you plan and deliver your presentation, and during the project period you should have some opportunities to practise for it. We will start with oral presentation.

Oral presentation

Giving an oral presentation, whether live or on video, can be daunting. Sometimes it can be easier if the audience is made up of people you know well (you are talking to friends so can relax); on the other hand, sometimes it is easier to address complete strangers (you can put on an act that is quite different from your usual shy self). Sometimes a prepared talk can be more effective than a display, as you have more scope to engage positively with a captive audience. Either way, you need to prepare carefully. In summary, the main tips are:

• Plan the content of your talk in some detail.

• Prepare some visual aids to help both your audience and yourself.

• Practise the talk out loud.

Activity 49 illustrates an important point about communicating information

ACTIVITY 49: THE RUMOUR CLINIC

Work in a group of at least five learners. One person will be told some information out of earshot of the rest. The first person must secretly tell the second what they have heard, who in turn tells the third person, and so on. At the end, compare the final and intermediate versions of the message with the original.

orally: however carefully you concentrate, it is very difficult to pick up information just by listening, particularly if you only hear it once. This has three important messages for the way you plan your presentation:

• keep it simple

• repeat key points

• use visual aids.

First, don't try to say too much. Concentrate on saying why you chose your topic, stating your point of view and summarising the main arguments and conclusion of your work. In a ten-minute talk, you will only have time to discuss, at most, two major points in any detail.

So, if something is really important, don't just say it once. Officers in the army are sometimes advised to "tell them what you're going to tell them, tell them, then tell them what you've told them" – in other words, introduction, main body and conclusion. Visual aids let your audience see the key points that you want them to take in. You may decide to use PowerPoint, an overhead projector, a blackboard or whiteboard, flip chart, posters, slides, video, or any combination of these to accompany your presentation. But whatever you choose, keep it simple. As a rough rule of thumb, use no more than one PowerPoint slide or overhead transparency for each minute of your talk – so that's ten maximum. And keep the content clear and simple too. People need to be able to take in the content at a glance, so write bullet points rather than continuous text, use a large font (at least 24 pt), and use just a few big clear pictures (Figure 5.2).

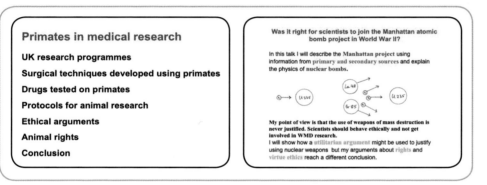

Figure 5.2 Good or bad examples of visual aids?

As well as helping your audience, your visual aids will help you stick to your planned structure without reading from notes. If you put each of your main points on a PowerPoint slide (or equivalent) then you will be reminded to talk in more detail about each in turn. Visual aids also support you by leading the audience to focus on the content of your talk rather than looking at you – this can be a great advantage if you are feeling a bit nervous.

ACTIVITY 50: TELLING A STORY

You will be given about five overhead transparencies in a random order. Decide how these can be arranged so as to tell a 'story'. Then use the transparencies to help you tell the story to other people.

5.2 Speaking well

One of the best ways to learn how to speak to an audience is to observe other people doing it. You can probably think of situations when you have been in the audience of a good, or a bad, speaker – either live (e.g. at school or college, in a public lecture, at a religious service) or while watching TV or video. Use these experiences to help you prepare for and practise your own oral presentation.

ACTIVITY 51: SPEAKING WELL, SPEAKING BADLY

In a small group, discuss your own experiences of being in the audience of good and bad speakers. List things that help keep you interested in what the speaker is saying, and things that make you switch off your attention.

Table 5.1 lists some things that you might have mentioned in Activity 50. You might be able to add some more.

Table 5.1 Speaking well, speaking badly

How to make your audience switch off	How to hold your audience's attention
Start your talk without looking at the audience	Begin by smiling at the audience
Read from notes	Talk to and look at the audience
Speak in a flat boring voice all the time	Vary your tone of voice
Speak very slowly all the time, or very quickly	Vary the pace. Avoid gabbling
Use a lot of unexplained technical jargon	Define any technical terms
Talk down to your audience	Use suitable language for you audience
Hunch your shoulders and keep your arms crossed.	Smile. Try to look relaxed
Say 'um' and 'er' a lot	Try not to 'um' and 'er'
Stare at a fixed point in the room	Skim the whole audience. Try to find some friendly faces to focus on in different parts of the room
Break off from the talk and spend a few minutes setting up your visual aids	Make sure all your visual aids are ready before you start, and that any equipment is working and you know how to use it
Fiddle with papers, hair, clothing, etc.	Hold a set of prompt cards
Ramble on without a break	Break up your talk into clear sections. Give the audience signals such as "first of all ... my next point is ... and finally"

If you don't have much experience of speaking to an audience, the right-hand column of Table 5.1 might make you think "easier said than done". But the main thing is to prepare carefully then smile at the audience, take some slow deep breaths and try to look relaxed. As with many things, speaking to an audience is something that improves with practice, so don't worry if at first you do find yourself 'umming' and 'erring' and speaking too fast. But do look for plenty of opportunities to practise before you give your main presentation.

The professionals

As you become more confident in speaking to an audience, you can begin to develop more techniques for grabbing people's attention and persuading them of your point of view. Actors, politicians and broadcasters (Figure 5.3) all have expertise in this, so watch them at work and see how they do it.

Figure 5.3
News presenters such as
Sir Trevor McDonald
are professional
communicators.

ACTIVITY 52: THE PROFESSIONALS

Watch a clip from a movie in which one of the characters makes an emotional speech (e.g. a scene from a courtroom drama). Analyse the speech by considering the following questions:

• Are there any facts presented in this speech?

• What opinions are given?

• Is there a clear, logical structure here?

• What is the speaker's argument and the conclusion?

• Pick out what is effective for the viewer/listener.

• Is it persuasive? If it is, try to identify what makes it so.

As you might have seen in Activity 51, a speech can sometimes be persuasive because of the way it is delivered as much as the content. When you make a presentation about your Project, you will be assessed on both content and delivery. So the message is: plan and prepare the content carefully, then try to communicate it as effectively as possible.

Planning your talk

Your presentation should take approximately ten minutes. In such a short time, you cannot attempt to describe everything that you did for your Project. Concentrate on talking about what you found out or produced, and the conclusions that you reached. Summarise your Research review and Development sections very briefly and choose one or perhaps two points to discuss in detail.

Start to plan your talk while you are working on the Discussion or Development section of your report. Then, when you have more or less finished the written report, spend some time on more detailed preparation for the presentation.

Plan what you are going to say in three parts.

Introduction (1 min)

This should take about 10 per cent of the allotted time (in this case, 1 minute). Try to find some way of grabbing people's attention immediately – perhaps display a picture or read a quotation, state an opinion or pose a question. Your introduction should be long enough to set the scene for the presentation but short enough to mark its own end clearly.

Main Body (7 and a half min)

The main 'meat' of your talk should take about 75 per cent of the time. You will need to be very selective – you cannot possibly communicate your entire Project in this short time.

Conclusion (1 and a half min)

Take about 15 per cent of your time to reinforce the 'take home' messages from your talk. Make sure you audience knows you are drawing to an end purposefully and not just stopping. Say "and finally...", sum up your main points, thank your audience and ask if they have any questions.

5.3 On display

As with an oral presentation, a display must be carefully planned. Think about what to include and how to tell the story of your Project. Don't try to include everything. To make sure you communicate the key points to your audience, you will have to pay attention to labelling and to the layout of your display. You might also consider providing a handout.

ACTIVITY 53: STOP AND LOOK

If possible, visit a professional display, e.g. in a museum. In a small group, discuss what you think makes a good or a poor display. Use the following questions to help focus your discussion.

- Is the display attractive? Do you feel drawn into it?

- Are objects and images used to good effect?

- What information is being presented?

- Are any labels or posters easy to read? Do they give too much information, or not enough?

- If the display tells a 'story', is it set out in a logical order?

Planning your display

Bearing in mind your discussion in Activity 53, think how you will design a display about your Project. You will need to think how best to display your Project, bearing in mind both what you want to communicate and the resources available.

Your Project

- What are the main points you want to communicate?

- Do you have any objects to display that are central to your Project (e.g. an artefact, apparatus used in an investigation)?

- Are there any other objects that would help tell the story of your work (e.g. sketchbooks, items used in a performance)?

- How can you use images? Do you have any photographs, diagrams or charts to display? How does each one contribute to the 'story' you want to tell?

- How can you best use text to convey information (e.g. labels on displayed items, posters)?

- Will you produce a handout for people who visit your display? What will it say? How can you ensure it is clear and easy to read?

Display space

- Where will you be setting up your display?

- How much room will you have?

- Will you be able to change the layout (e.g. move furniture around)?

- Will there be display boards? How big are they? How are things to be attached to them?

- Will there be tables or floor space where you can display objects?

- What lighting will be available (e.g. normal room lights, spotlights)?

- What technical resources will be available (e.g. plasma screen, data projector, sound system)?

It is a good idea to look at the display space well in advance. Make a sketch of the space, measure and record its dimensions, and note any key features (such as fire doors that must be unobstructed).

Select one item (such as a piece of apparatus, drama prop or photograph) that is relevant to your Project. On a sheet of A3 paper, make a poster that gives some information about the item and explains why it is important. Write bullet points rather than chunks of text, and use a large font. The poster can include images as well as text, but make sure it does not look cluttered.

Display the item and the poster, and invite comments and questions from other members of your class.

5.4 Seminar

Work in progress

During your work on your Project, you will probably be asked to take part in one or more seminars (Figure 5.4). The purpose of these seminars is to help you to clarify your thinking about your Project, to receive advice from your teacher/tutor and other learners, and to contribute your advice to other people's work. Academic researchers, be they scientists, historians, philosophers, or from other subject areas, often take part in such seminars for precisely the same purposes. If you are working on a performance, seminars will probably take the form of group meetings where you review progress and each person talks about their own contribution and how it relates to what everyone else is doing.

Figure 5.4 Work in progress seminar

ACTIVITY 55: WORK IN PROGRESS

Plan, prepare and deliver a short oral presentation on one aspect of your Project. Raise any questions relating to your Project that you would find it helpful to discuss. Respond to questions from the rest of the class, and listen to other people's comments and suggestions.

In a seminar, you will be asked to give a short presentation on some aspect of your work in progress. This might be a report on some literature sources that you have been consulting, an update on your laboratory or fieldwork, a demonstration of how your artefact is being developed, or a discussion of some arguments relevant to your topic. Whichever is the case, you need to prepare to speak for a few minutes to the rest of your class and to respond to questions. This is also an opportunity for you to ask questions and gather other people's views on aspects of your Project. If you are wondering how best to move your work forward, other people's suggestions and comments can be very valuable.

Use seminars as an opportunity to practise and develop your presentation skills. Plan what you will say, and prepare some suitable visual aids. This will be valuable when you come to give your main presentation – you will probably be able to adapt or reuse what you have prepared earlier.

Questions and discussion

Responding to questions will be an important part of your final presentation, so any experience gained beforehand will be helpful. 'Question time' (Figure 5.5) can be more daunting than the rest of your presentation because you cannot prepare for it in the same way, but the following points are worth bearing in mind.

Figure 5.5 Question time

- You will almost certainly know more about your Project than anyone else in the room, including your teacher/tutor.

- The more interesting your presentation, the more questions people will ask. So take every question as a compliment, even if the questioner is disagreeing with you.

- Pause for thought before launching into an answer – particularly if you are not sure what to say.

- If you don't know the answer to a question, be honest and say so.

- If someone asks about an aspect of your Project that has not previously occurred to you, be grateful. It might be something worth looking into as your Project develops.

- Keep your answers short so as to give several people a chance to ask questions.

- Try not to let one person dominate. Try to take questions from a range of people.

- If someone persists in demanding a more detailed response to their question, offer to discuss it with them privately afterwards.

- Be polite if someone tries to put you down; don't enter into an argument. Try to use phrases such as "that's an interesting point of view" or "well, that's a different way of looking at things" or "that's something I'll have to think about".

Do unto others...

Listening to other people's presentations and asking them questions is an important aspect of taking part in a seminar. When someone else is giving a presentation, try to imagine yourself in their situation and behave as you would wish your own audience to behave. In short:

- Remember, the speaker may be nervous even if they don't look it.

- Listen to the presentation with respect.

- Try to think of a constructive question to ask – and listen attentively to the answer.

ACTIVITY 56: REFLECTION   RL

After the seminar, reflect on how it went for you. Start by trying to think of the good points, then think of aspects that you can work to improve next time. Your teacher/tutor will probably be able to give you some helpful feedback.

5.5 Presentation

Be prepared

After you have finished the written report of your Project, you can focus your attention fully on your presentation.

You will be told the date and time in advance. Make sure you are well prepared in good time.

For an oral presentation

Make sure you:

• plan the content and timing of your talk carefully

• prepare your visual aids

• practise giving your presentation to an audience.

For the first two of these, refer to previous lessons for guidance and draw on the experience that you have built up during your work on your Project. When you are fairly sure you have prepared a more or less final version of your presentation, hold a dress rehearsal. Ideally, the dress rehearsal will take place in the same room as your final presentation, in front of a small audience of learners from your class (Figure 5.6).

Figure 5.6 Dress rehearsal.

For a display

Make sure you:

• plan the content and layout of your display carefully

• prepare all your materials

• check that your planned layout fits into the space available.

Planning

When planning your presentation, it is useful to keep in mind the same '5 W' questions (and one H) that you have met in the context of gathering information:

• *What*: make your theme statement

• *Why*: state your purpose clearly

• *When*: know the time you are presenting, and any time that will be available beforehand, e.g. for setting up your display or familiarising yourself with the technology

Divine command For people with a religious faith, right conduct is often seen as fulfilling what is required by divine command. These commands are generally revealed in holy scriptures and the teachings of a specialised group of people, such as priests or imams.

Duties Things each of us ought to do. For example, if you have a child, you have a duty to look after him or her.

Ethical frameworks Conceptual structures that allow a person to decide the rightness or wrongness of actions. Standard ethical frameworks include utilitarianism, rights and duties, and virtue ethics.

Ethics Reasoned views about why certain things are morally wrong and other things are morally right.

Evidence A means of proving an unknown or disputed fact, or supporting a point of view. Well established facts and primary sources of information provide much more compelling evidence than secondary sources, subjective opinion or speculation.

Fact A statement about which there is no uncertainty or dispute. For example, it is a fact that Tony Blair became UK Prime Minister in 1997, and that light travels in a vacuum at 300 million metres per second.

Gantt chart A two-dimensional planning and review chart named after Henry Gantt (1861–1919) in which each task is represented by a timeline indicating its start and end time and other key stages. The timelines are all displayed in parallel against a common time-scale.

Hypothesis An 'educated guess' at an explanation, usually based on observation or experiment. A scientific hypothesis often gives rise to propositions that can be tested by further experiment or observation.

Invalid An invalid argument is one in which the conclusion does not follow from the premises. If an argument is invalid, it is possible for the premises to be true, but the conclusion false.

Materialism The view that the human being is made up of physical stuff alone: there is no non-physical mind or soul.

Mind map A chart showing the relationships between ideas.

Morals Beliefs about which things are right and which are wrong. For example, a person might believe that hunting animals for their fur is always wrong but that eating meat is acceptable provided that the animals from which the meat comes do not suffer.

Objections The same as *counter-arguments*.

Objective Unaffected by a person's emotions, sensations or beliefs. Facts are objective (whereas opinions are subjective).

Opinion Someone's personal judgement about what seems to be true. For example, it is a matter of opinion whether Margaret Thatcher was a good prime minister, or whether chocolate is delicious.

Peer review In Science and other academic disciplines, the process by which people's work is checked by others with knowledge of the field before publication.

PERT chart (Program Evaluation and Review Technique) A two-dimensional planning and review chart in which each task is represented by an arrow labelled with its duration. Arrows drawn end-to-end indicate which tasks must be performed in sequence, and branches in the network of arrows indicate which tasks can be performed independently of one another.

Philosophy The discipline in which fundamental ideas are discussed, with the aim of understanding these ideas more clearly and thinking critically about the reasons people give for their fundamental beliefs.

Plagiarism Using someone else's work and pretending it is your own. Plagiarism occurs whenever someone's work is used without being acknowledged. A scientist copying someone else's results, a student buying an essay from a website and a writer quoting from a book without giving the source are all committing plagiarism.

Points of view Beliefs about philosophical (or ethical) matters.

Premises The starting points for an argument. (When an argument is presented, the premises are not necessarily placed at the beginning.)

Primary source A record produced during an event, or by someone who was present when it happened. A scientist's lab notebook and a video recording are both examples of primary sources. Historians generally prefer to use primary sources as they give a more direct record of an event than secondary sources. But primary sources might still be subject to bias, for example, when someone involved in an event is not aware of all the facts or wishes to promote a particular interpretation.

Proposition In philosophy, arguments are used to provide support for particular propositions. For example, the 'first cause' argument is designed to establish the proposition that God exists.

Realism The view of those who (unlike relativists) believe that there is an objective reality which our theories try to describe.

Reasons Statements that provide support for a point of view.

Relativism The view of those who (unlike realists) believe that truth is relative: it depends upon your point of view. Moral relativism is the view that maintains that nothing is absolutely right or wrong (i.e. right or wrong at all times, in all places and in all circumstances). The context can mean that any action normally considered wrong (e.g. telling lies, being sexually unfaithful, even torture or murder) may be justifiable.

Rights Things that should nearly always be allowed. Most people believe that humans have such rights as the right to life, the right to freedom of speech, the right to a fair trial and so on. Under certain circumstances a person may lose a right – for example, you don't have the right to freedom of speech if that means shouting 'fire' in a crowded public place when there is no fire. If someone has a right to something, it usually means that one or more people have duties to that person.

Secondary source A record produced after an event by someone who was not present. An encyclopedia entry and a TV documentary are examples of secondary sources. Secondary sources rely on other sources of information, some of which might be primary sources.

Soul The non-physical essential part of a human being, according to the dualist point of view.

Speculation Guessing what might happen or what might have happened, or the reasons why an event or action took place.

Subjective Affected by a person's emotions, sensations or beliefs. Opinions are subjective (whereas facts are objective).

Timeline A one-dimensional chart showing dates on or by which certain actions should be, or were, carried out, or dates on which certain events took place.

Theism The belief in the existence of a god.

Thought experiment An imaginary scenario used to test how our concepts work in cases completely unlike those in which we normally use them.

Utilitarianism The ethical framework which holds that the right course of action is that which maximises the amount of happiness or pleasure in the world. If you are a utilitarian it means that while you might, for example, normally respect other people's property, there could be occasions when you would believe that the right thing to do would be to steal.

Valid A valid argument is one in which the conclusion follows from the premises. In a valid argument it is not possible for the premises to be true and the conclusion false.

Virtue ethics Ethical framework that stresses the development of good character traits, i.e. virtues. Precisely what the virtues are is open to disagreement, and may vary from place to place and at different times in history. However, certain virtues, such as kindness and courage, are valued by most cultures.

Index